# Poems
## That
# Provoke
# Thought

BY
LENVEL E. HALE

iUniverse, Inc.
New York   Bloomington

# Poems that Provoke Thought

*iUniverse books may be ordered through booksellers or by contacting:*

*iUniverse*
*1663 Liberty Drive*
*Bloomington, IN 47403*
*www.iuniverse.com*
*1-800-Authors (1-800-288-4677)*

*Because of the dynamic nature of the Internet, any Web addresses or links contained in this book may have changed since publication and may no longer be valid. The views expressed in this work are solely those of the author and do not necessarily reflect the views of the publisher, and the publisher hereby disclaims any responsibility for them.*

*ISBN: 978-1-4401-1628-5 (pbk)*
*ISBN: 978-1-4401-1629-2 (ebk)*

*Printed in the United States of America*

*iUniverse rev. date: 4/1/2009*

# A Baptism Tonight

A call came over the phone today.
Transferring a message of happiness on the way.
A young man had chosen to make a commitment from sin.
A move to change his life was to begin.
Happiness, yet sadness came over me.
For many concerns were mine to see.
Joy I felt for the desire to confess.
Yet, sorrow, for someone had failed a test.
The test of love for the future of a soul.
Had been missed and allowed disappointment to unfold.
A first day of the week service I attended that night.
To watch a young man move from darkness to light.
In his mind he felt welcome amongst those he knew.
For in his past others had lost the point of view.
In times past he had attended a church of the sign.
Yet, had felt rejection in the actions of mankind.
The church with the sign once had a chance to win.
But something happened, and they lost in the end.
Whether it was animosity, anger, or just plain greed.
A soul moved from the Sabbath to a first day need.
How many have been lost from the day sat aside?
To a religion whose change can't be denied.
Yes, I saw a baptism in the first day trend.
And I'm sad that the Sabbath lost in the end.
I'm filled with questions coming to mind.
When was it that their light failed to shine?
When one falters in their actions toward another.
The domino effect goes from one to the other.
When sight is lost and one loses control.
Friction amongst the brothers can cause the loss of a soul.

Where does fault belong? The church had its chance.
To treat a visitor in a way their love would enhance.
Actions and deeds will be placed before us one day.
And it will be too late for them to change their way.
We must examine ourselves from outside to within.
And repair anything that would cause one to sin.
We must look at each with the desire to win.
And do what is necessary to encourage the Sabbath trend.
For how can the Sabbath church continue to grow?
If to the first day worship it causes one to go.

# A Beautiful Prayer

I heard a beautiful prayer that was spoken to God today.
It was filled with fine words with only good things to say.
It was spoken as a request for help, in the trials of life's way.
Yes, it was a beautiful prayer that was spoken today!
I heard a prayer today. It was an appeal to God for help.
It was a call to the Creator. A request that was deeply felt.
It was a plea to the Master. Asking to act without delay.
Yes, it was a beautiful prayer, that was spoken today!
Its author was speaking for a group with words of his own.
Trying to say the things necessary, with all sincerity shown.
Asking for the granting of desires, from the one above.
All done in hope an answer would come as a sign of love.
Putting words in the right perspective, and in a special way.
Yes, it was a beautiful prayer that was spoken today!
Words of earnest, in asking were the thoughts at hand.
A solemn plea for help, in the trials and temptations of man.
It was a humble action to God, and to beg if need be.
As a child to a parent. Asking these things for you and me.
Some words though were lost, and a few I could barely hear.
As music from the instruments, continued to reach my ear.
As the Creator looked down on the group, that were trying to pray.
I hope He will grant their wishes, and not just say.
Yes, it was a beautiful prayer that was spoken today!

# A Father and his son

I'll strive to be a guide throughout your youthful years.
Always ready to help drive away little fears.
A sincere promise, Cause that's how it should be
Between a father and his son.
As you face the darkness of a long winter night.
I'll be there to serve, as your guiding light.
As you learn, from your adventures of choice.
I'll provide the foundation for you to rejoice.
As Christ is my leader in showing the way.
I too, will walk beside you every day.
As you mature into manhood, and my work is done.
I know you will also reach out to your little one.
Whether in body or spirit, I'll stand by your side.
So my love for you can never be denied.
That's how is should be
Between a father and his son.
As Christ is my guiding light toward the future of man.
I pray my example will cause you to hold his hand.
Always in thought, we two should be one.
That's how it should be between a father and his son.

# A Friend gone astray

A sharp pain went through me today.
As I touched the hand of a friend gone astray.
I hurt from my head to the tip of my toe.
As I heard words excepting the woe.
It's hard to understand one saying to me.
No hope, nor rejoicing, for in heaven I'll never be!
The pain wasn't as though it came from a knife.
Yet it cut deep, because of the absence of life.
The words perched my soul to the depths within.
And had more impact than the swords of men.
When hope is lost, then life is gone.
There is nothing left but time alone.
To refuse the gift Christ has gave.
Is to live with nothing left but the grave.
How sad it must be to put eternal life aside.
And enclose within, all feelings to hide.
Life  has to be of the greatest sorrow.
With the loss of hope when there is no tomorrow.
How can one come to such a state as this?
In order to say "eternal life I've missed"
How can one draw themselves so deep inside?
To the point that God has been denied.
Forgetting that He forgives those who honestly pray.
And promises to take their sorrows away.
Many times it's hard to get burdens to lift.
Yet, through faith we can have the promised gift.
Don't let life's problems bring you to despair.
Lift up your eyes to the one who cares.
For we have the sacrificed blood of the lamb.
Who is the Son sent from the great I AM.

The blood on the door post is for me and you.
All we have to do is have faith, and remain true.
Truly, it's hard for the one that feels alone.
Especially if from a brother, love is not shown.
So if you have a brother that is down and blue.
Let no part in losing his life belong to you.
Give a helping hand with joy in what you say.
And work to see them again on judgment day!
Always work and pray as you travel life's way.
And never be a cause, for anyone to go astray!

# A reason to live

Oh, for the many wishes to have never been born.
No feeling of this misery, no trials to be won.
From the eerie deep, I could be in a place of the unknown.
I could lay in darkness where nothing is shown.
In the deepest of sleep, I could forever be.
Never to see light, nor have someone laugh with me.
These are thoughts that always rush through my mind.
I am lonely and in despair almost all the time.
But then I hear a soft voice rush through me.
"Yesterday is gone". Today's beauty you should see.
What joy you could find as from sleep you awake.
To see the sunrise as it reflects upon a lake.
To hear the songs of the birds amongst the trees.
To feel your waving hair caused by the gentle breeze.
The beauty of life itself with all its splendor shown.
From the darkness all this I could have never known.
No eyes could be more privileged than these of mine.
To behold the handy work that makes the sun to shine.
No hands should be more thankful than mine should be.
To reach for a mate to pull very close to me.
No feet should be happier, carrying me here and there.
Walking beside another as life's ups and down we share.
These ears I have are a miracle this I know is true.
Because they allow me to hear the words "I love you"
These are things never felt by one not yet born.
Nor are they heard by one that chooses to be alone.

Yes, one could choose the darkness of a pit.
Or choose life, and the joys that come with it.
But life does not come without ups and downs.
Joy comes from defeating temptations that abound.
But privileges we have are for all the creation to see.
This has to make life worth while for you and me.
That's why it's great to have these things I feel.
Without life, all these could never have been real.
I'm reminded in the darkness I would forever be alone.
For that is a place joy and love never can be shown.
Yet, I live and many things I know can be mine.
Many friends, many joys, all in their due time.
As I look around and put the dark thoughts away.
There appears a new world at the dawning of the day.
When the veil is removed there's always a helping hand.
So much can be offered during our life's span.
But one must move from darkness to the light.
For one is life and the other eternal night.
Life's greatest moments are in making a new start.
And the joy of this life is just a smaller part.
All of life, here with its beauty that's so grand.
Is a sample to be experienced in another land.
All the sayings I have listed are what I now give.
They are the wonders of life, and the reasons to live.

# Are you free from Habitual Sin?

Have you bowed at the alter to confess your sins?
And stated that your hearts desire is to make amends.

Have you vowed to God you will learn a new way?
Yet, have several problems moving from sin every day.

As you look for His instructions in order to make a change.
Do you face the ability of choosing as very strange?

Is there a war always going on in your soul?
The constant battle with self in forming a new mold.

Becoming Spiritual is a must in the view of God.
Otherwise, chastisement will follow with a rod.

It's hard to change from a thorn to the rose.
And sometimes one wonders about the path chose.

But constantly checking self will produce a good thing.
And it's worth the effort along with the pain.

Though we try to make it through each day.
It is very often that we falter and sway.

Yet, to train ourselves to walk the straight line.
Will take much effort and maybe a life time.

Yet, we can not continue to repeat wrongs every day.
To do so is to eventually abandon Gods way.

# As the waters flow freely

As the waters flow freely over the ground,
in their path to the sea.
The waters of life flow from Christ to you and me.
And if one opens their heart to allow
themselves to be covered with love.
Their cup will be completely filled with the eternal waters
from above.

# Bee Hive

Look at how the tree limb covers the bees,
As a hen would cover her chicks in the nest.
Giving an example of how Gods hand covers as we go through life's test.
The God who cares for the Sparrow and gives the fields for their meal.
Will always provide us with the things necessary
In order to maintain our seal.

# Bewildered

I am just a little bewildered Lord on how you answer prayers.
Especially when I ask you to protect me in my dares.
I ask you before going on a trip to plant your seed.
And I cover as much territory as possible though I sometimes speed.
Sad I was when I got the ticket for doing 80 in a 60 zone.
But after seeing those others, I really didn't feel alone.
Remember the time I prayed for you to protect my boat from theft?
I know I left it on the street, but I had no storage left.
And the many times I prayed for you to keep my child from harm.
Yet, he became really sick, after drinking poison I left in the barn.
I realize I should have put it up, after I sprayed the yard.
But after all that work I really felt too tired.
Lord I am now praying for good health each and every day.
Though I eat anything I want, and cook it just anyway.
Lord it becomes a confusing thing when I find.
You won't perform a miracle to protect each move of mine.
I thought you would take control of events I put in the way.
And overlook my un-concern that I make almost every day.
You say I'm looking at this from the wrong point of view?
And you expect me to do something before depending on you.
Are you telling me it takes a little effort on my part?
That I should do something before asking you to start.
Jimminee crickets Lord, I guess I have this thing all wrong.
I thought you would perform miracles to help me get along.
Now I find you require me to follow rules to keep myself from harm,
And after that, you will extend your helping arm!
You know what Lord?

Maybe I'm not the only one that depends too much on you.
Maybe many have forgot you require us to first do what we should do.
And after we have practiced safety, obeyed your laws, and loved our fellowman.
Then, we can call on you and know we have your helping hand!
I believe I've got to stop and take another look at how I pray.
And then I can be assured you will be with me every day.

# Bind Us Together

A cloth is made as the weaver takes the task.
Fitting them together, making beauty for one to ask.
Parts are not as valuable when standing alone.
Binding together causes a master piece to be born.
Such are you and I in the things we have chosen to do.
Apart we struggle; together the oneness will carry us through.
The binding together is the strength needed for us to be one.
And strength is a must for the cause of Christ to be won.
Therefore build a thing of beauty for everyone to see.
And binding together in love is joy for you and me.
In the love of Christ there is no duty we can not master.
Yes, bind us together now and once again in our life after.

# Could you?

Could you - For a moment, close your eyes and let several thoughts go
through your mind?
And visualize the wonders you've witnessed in your life time.

Could you – With your knowledge, allow yourself to roam from star to star?
And dream for a little while about the Universe and the place where you are.

Could you – Picture yourself standing on the moon and looking down at
the Earth? And even imagine what would be its net worth.

Could you – For just a minute, conceive in your thoughts a price that you
would give? Or even the amount one would pay just to continue to live.

Could you – View in your thoughts a thing worth more than what you see?
And really realize the possibility that someone is you and me.

Could you – Ever imagine a demonstration having to take place, to show us
the value of the human race?

Could you – Really convince yourself that our value was purchased by love?
And how it could be possible this love came from above.

Could you – Learn that for us, money has no purchasing power? And could
you allow yourself to accept the fact it took a life during the final hour?

Could you – Depend on your belief that it was Gods Son that was sent?
And have the faith that it was "The Christ" whose life was spent.

Could you – Put your faith in the story you have had unfold? And believe
we could have eternal life forever to hold?

Could you – Answer yes to all these questions today,
And know the value our Savior agreed to pay?

Could you – Realize that His gem of the universe places second best. For
those who are willing and able to pass the test?

# Crystal Clear Water

The crystal clear water of
life is not only found in the streams
flowing so free.
But the water of eternal life is found in
Jesus, the Christ!
Flowing for you and me.

# Dad

While young and growing, as parents doing your part.
Working hard, laboring long, and providing to give a start.
Training a child I know now, was not easy at all.
I have two, and in life, I know they will stand tall.
After growing up, you and I had no time together.
But a hidden love for each other will last forever.
The fate of time, stopped us and cut short our days.
Though the last years together, I will remember always.
Though you are not here now, I know you'll be there.
I trust and believe God answered our last prayer.
What time we had together, oh I am so glad.
A meeting here, with friendship and love to share.
Oh how I miss you "dad!"

# Death is always near

A wonder of life, the birth of a child one must say.
While right beside it, death is in the way.

Watching as from a baby to a youthful one, we continue to know.
That lingering in the dark is death waiting to show.

To a young adult we soon become, as time continues to go by.
And through the mistakes and near misses, death is very sly.

Though somehow we obtain adulthood and learn to guide our step.
The lingering of death continues by our side, for it has never left.

Throughout our life in all matter of toils and strife.
We will find that death has been waiting to take our life.

The fear of the unknown is just on the other side of the dark.
For the mind can not grasp the reality of things after we part.

This question has been raised by man since the time he sinned
He was told there was life on the other side after death came in.

But this life is only for those found worthy to have it given.
To those whose fear of death is overcome by desires to keep living.

And this after life is one for doing the will of God Himself.
And is granted to those who believe no more death is left.

# Faith

I have a little something I would like to talk about.
We used to have a lot of it to make us jump and shout.

It was something we had to work on in order for it to build.
It was something that got bigger as we saw the things so real.

We used to carry it with us as we went to and fro.
Now we don't have as much to take wherever we go.

Somehow we have lost the full cup we once had.
Maybe we have half of it and it should make one very sad.

We loose more and more as on a human we depend.
If we are not careful we will loose it all in the end.

This thing I speak of is most important for all I know.
For without it, to be with the lord we can never go.

We are told to keep it and always have it near.
I know, without it I would always be lost in fear.

Somehow we must gain that which we have lost.
It will take a lot, but we have to pay the cost.

For without it we can never stand at the Saviors door.
Yes, without our Faith We will be lost forever more.

# For I even I

I know he will abide with me till the end.
His love for me I can always depend.
Always staying near to guide me home.
He will never go away and leave me alone.

He gave his life for sinners like me.
So that for us eternal life could be.
Why not this one what hove you to loose?
What more of a friend could anyone choose?

Accept this one called Christ today.
Oh please listen to what I have to say.
Your life may stop any time you know.
Then what will you have of love to show.

This inter-peace is what we need.
And it is only him that gives peace indeed
Come now my friend accept his loving way.
And gain that gift of eternal life today.

For I, even I, have a light that glows.
For I, even I, have a light to shows.
His love for me will always be.
And I, even I, have the gift you see.

# Forever

You have heard the word forever, and how it's used for you and me.
But did you know it has meanings that are not easy to believe?
There are thoughts of it having a meaning as far as time can tell.
And in other statements it can make some wonder about doing well!
But forever, as God said it, has not changed throughout the years.
Though some are not sure, yet others see it as it really appears.
Can you imagine time without day or night, to measure the way?
Or the Sun and Moon, to never rise or set to mark another day?
Can you conceive in thought, how time will stand still to move no more?
To allow one to exist in peace and harmony upon a distant shore.
Time we will not be able to find, that  causes the years to pass.
For the pleasures in working for the Creator will be our duty at last.
When we look at our life that is counted quickly by the passing of time.
Can we visualize no day or night, and only peace occupying the mind?
The human mind can not conceive, how one can pass from death to life.
To move to a land that is absent of all known sorrow and strife.
And it's hard to believe a God, would grant to us such a wonderful gift.
When we are just a tiny speck in the universe that has been set adrift.
Forever, have you ever thought what the word really means to you?
Can you think in your mind the reality of this word being true?
Can you believe that forever is a state with no day or night?
That it is a place of joy, where the Son of God is the light?
For that light shall be provided through out all eternity.
By the Son of God in the state of forever, for all to see.
Yes, forever is eternity without time with no other meaning to apply.
So increase your trust to be with our Creator, forever in the after life.

# Fruit on the vine

The fruit hangs from the vine waiting to turn sweet.
As the nutrients assemble to make it ready to eat.

## THE CREATOR!

Provides the food of life for each man, woman, and child.
Requiring only that one walk with Him that extra mile.

# God Bless America    "In God We Trust"

These are words we really like to hear.
Words our forefathers set about to have them near.
They were written and many were spoken.
Hoping that trust would never be broken.
Striving to worship a God! once denied by a land of oppress.
Where Freedom was never enjoyed, yet a desire for rest.
Freedom! Freedom! Was their constant cry.
So strong that it caused many to die.
Thrown into prisons, and beaten with a rod.
Just for trying to serve this God.
Giving their lives to break away, and come across the sea.
To find a land of peace, to be happy and free.
GOD BLESS AMERICA! A cry that rang loud.
No fear was felt, for God was their guarding cloud.
And to show trust in the one they could not see.
An insignia was placed on all the currency.
Truly, there was no better place for this sign to be.
For the Creator had given them this land of the free.
God will be on our side in all we say and do!
Yes, God is on our side and He will lead us through.
This was the feeling some two hundred years ago.
But what would our fathers do, if they could see our story unfold?
We proclaim how to God we are true.
Yet, allow our schools to remove the golden rule!
We go to church and stand tall, one day a week.
Yet when they say no prayer in school, we do not speak!
We will not make a move for the others to see.
Yet, we continue to thank God for our being free.
Yes, GOD BLESS AMERICA! This is what we want.
But! "God in our Government," and we say "don't".

Slowly they are removing our Creator from all activity.
Soon we will be like the land left across the sea.
The leaders of old did not keep "God" at home.
For in all their activities they brought Him along.
Now we are removing Him from all but our once-a-week place.
Therefore I ask, "How long will He stay in the race?"
How can the "God" of our forefathers help us stay free?
When in the nation's activities we won't let Him be.
Soon the words "God bless America" will not be heard.
And if we are not careful, others will burn His word.
"GOD BLESS AMERICA" - great are the words from our past!
Words our forefathers truly expected to last.
So let this thought go ringing through your ear.
If we won't let Him lead our actions.
"How can we expect Him to stay near?"

# Hard Rules

My father told me when I was young. Son, save your money now.
And when you get older you will have enough to provide for your retirement.
I believed my father, but I did not save money.
Today I do not have much put aside.
The system tells me he was right.
For many did save and today they have a lot.
He also told me that if I applied myself I could learn a good trade.
I again believed him and studied hard. And today I know five
different trades. What he said was again true.
The difference is that even though I believed him about the money.
I did not act upon that belief, and therefore, I did not obtain the end
result. On the second advice, I believed him, and I did act.
And I was able to do what I sat out to do. Thus proving that I had to act
in order to show my faith!
When I did, then, I was rewarded because of my actions.
Believing someone (trust in what is
said) was not good enough. Neither of the two would have
just come my way if I had sat down and waited.
(thus proving faith without works is dead)

---

Once upon a time there was a rule with a meaning so tight.
To the wrong it was a burden, but to the righteous a delight.
You shall have no other Gods! Was the call to people below.
And the penalty for idol worship was a sad thing to behold.
Do not steal! Covet! Or kill! The things the neighbors hold dear.
To the righteous, there was no problem. To evil there was fear.
Remember the Sabbath day! For your God has sat it aside.
It's good to rest and worship, this can't be denied.
There were more rules given, and all to provide a code.
And the opposition cried aloud. These are to heavy a load!

We can't obey all these words!  For He has given too much!
Though for the good of man these had the master's touch.
Again the opposition calls and reasons once or twice.
We can make these rules easy, by giving ourselves advice!
Advice they gave while explaining the meaning of each.
The rules were not so bad for us; it's just that they are out of reach.
No one has to follow the rules of old.  For now they are replaced.
Don't worry about obedience; just be thankful for His grace.
They say, just do the best you can, and He will do the rest.
Depend upon the love of Christ, and you will pass the test.
In times of old one had to have faith and work a little too!
But now it's said that all one must do, is obey the golden rule.
Love thy neighbor as thyself is what is said to me.
But what good is love if one doesn't act for others to see?
Love God with all your being, is first to be in your heart.
But how can one show this love, If His rules we have no part?
The rules to His children have no binding; this is what we are told.
But only those not understanding, claim they have no hold.
Believing in Christ is not the only thing for life we must do.
For believing is not enough, it also requires one to follow a rule.
Why is it man would like these things to go away?
Is it to do as he feels and be able to have his say?
If we aren't careful, and the rules we continue to deny.
We will find ourselves without a foundation on which we can rely.
And with no foundation for our faith which is in Jesus Christ
We will find ourselves standing alone, without a Sacrifice.

# Have you had the seed of hate?

Have you ever had an ache that went to the bottom of your soul?
Have you ever had a feeling for which you had no control?
Have you said and done the things one ought not do?
Have you found yourself having trouble obeying the golden rule?
Have you felt the desire to rip away at a person you do not like?
To have things come across your mind in which Christ has no delight!
Have you ever felt that no one was on your side?
And you wish there was some place you could run and hide.
Have you felt the anger turn to hate to the point of despair?
Finding fault in every thing another has to share.
Have you ever wondered why these things happen to us?
Is it possible it is a seed planted deep inside our dust?
That causes one to feel self is the only one to trust.
Is it possible that seed is of the dangerous kind?
And because of it, our real value has no chance to shine.
Is it possible that seed is hate because of a past deed or wise?
And will always prevent the renewing of our former ties!
Is it wise for one to cast all of the good away;
And allow the seed of hate to invade every day?
Though it's true, and yet one will not believe.
Having the seed of hate, eternal life one can not receive.
Life should be the greatest, while present on this earth.
But the seed of hate, will prevent the new birth.
Consider these things said, in hope thoughts will come alive.
And rid the seed of hate, so that the second death you may survive.

# His Name

They tell me that through the years His name has been lost.
And today one cannot find it no matter what the cost.

And when one tries to bring His identity to light.
There are those who will work hard in the fight.

To keep it hidden and pressed deep from view.
So that it will be hard to deliver to me and you.

From the beginning of time in the garden of life.
His name was known amongst the strife.

But as time went on and the beguilement came.
The evil one worked hard in removing His name.

Until today it is very seldom from people heard.
Though it is written many times in the recorded word.

The beguilement is strong amongst the religions of today.
In the efforts by the leaders to form an absolute sway.

Failing to look at the evidence given by Him.
That He intended to be known above other gods by men.

The penalty may be great to those who claim to be right.
Not knowing His identity, they may spend eternity in the night.

Is He just God to man without the identity power?
And will man be lost to call on Him in the final hour?

When man is faced with the leaving of his life giving flow.
How can one call on whom they do not know?

# How are you going to know it is He?

Come Lord! Why do you delay?
I know by the signs it's close to the day.
Come Lord! For I have remained true.
I have all my things together, and I'm waiting for you!
These are words spoken by many of those around.
Is it a true feelings being expressed, or just voicing a sound?
Are you really ready to go at any time?
Are your bags packed, amends made, waiting for the Son to shine?
**But how are you going to know it is He?**
**How are you going to know it is He?**
How is one to know when the Lord has set His feet upon the earth?
When He said to watch for others claiming to offer the new birth.
Oh I know! Some will say.
There will be a war like none from then until today.
Or, there will be a light coming from the east and the heavens will melt away.
Lightening shall strike and thunder shall roar.
And the Lord shall come to rule forever more.
**But how are you going to know it is He?**
**How are you going to know it is He?**
When He comes He will rule with a fist of iron and a rod of steel!
That's how I am going to know which one is really real.
Another expression of hopefulness, coming from the earthly kind.
Which is just another event listed as a tattle tale sign.
So many signs, so many thoughts, are expressed everywhere.
It's as though everyone has the secret, and waiting for it to share.
These many things people of today truly hold very near.
Mystery's that confound the world, while waiting for Him to appear.
**But how are you going to know it is He?**
**How are you going to know it is He?**

No matter how you understand His appearance.

There is something one must never allow to slip.

**"Faith and Obedience",** and always ready to make the trip.

Whether in silent clouds or shouts of acclimation.

If from Death you arise to be,

**Then you will know it is He? Yes you will know it is He?**

# How would you feel?

How would you feel knowing God would not answer your prayer?

Would you continue to ask, or would you even dare?

How would you feel if you knew you were hated by another?

Would you try to solve the problem, or say "hi" and go no farther?

How would you feel if you said vain words to a friend today?

Would you just wave your hands and let him go his way?

How would you feel knowing you had sin on your heart?

Would you pretend nothing was wrong and never make a new start?

How would you feel if you were to die today?

Knowing the sin you have, had not been taken away.

How would you feel having ought against your brother for his ways?

Could it put you in the same condition as the one gone astray?

How would you feel knowing in Gods word it has always been.

To not forgive a brother is to remain in sin?

How would you feel, with the burden on your mind.

And not getting it relieved, before the end of time?

And how would you feel if before Christ on judgment day?

He looked at you and said, "I never knew you, go away!"

# I don't want to learn anymore

Here he is once again! Came to hear words from the preacher man!
To say "yes!", "amen" that's good! And let him know how he will stand.
Once a week he gathers there with the thoughts of praising God.
And when new is presented, He is quick to move his head with a nod.
He feels he knows enough to keep a watch on his hearts door.
Therefore he feels no need to really learn anymore.

He has the desire to live from week to week, and let his light shine.
But to alter or change his life, he just will not allow the time.
The Scriptures are his;   He has read them again and again.
And sometimes a new light will shine concerning the area of sin.
But to change his actions and turn about, this he would deplore.
For He knows enough already, and doesn't want to learn anymore.

To hear he may have been wrong, on how God's word should flow.
Makes him ask the question.  Just how much do I need to know?
And when someone tells of a new thing that has just been learned.
Fear comes, for if he listens, his life will have to take a turn.
He's sure to keep these disturbances from his hearts door.
He has made up his mind, He just won't learn anymore.

He hears someone speak with words different than what he's been taught.
And quickly moves to blot them out, considering their value naught.
He ignores the Holy Spirit that communicates in many different ways.
Though directed throughout history from the ancient of days.
No matter how much the Creator reveals, he will not open his hearts door.
But will keep it tightly closed, because he doesn't want to learn anymore.

When we gather together to study, and learn how God is speaking to man.
We should not let a closed heart be the method of our stand.
But hear each word as though, it was a message coming to the ear.
For one never knows when the Spirit is trying to get us to hear.
We can't go through life feeling, we have enough knowledge in store.
Nor with the thoughts of " I don't want to learn anymore".
What's going to happen as time passes by and life comes to an end?
How will he feel, seeing he could have learned to remove that little sin?
How is it going to be when a finger is pointed on that day?
And He says "You could have learned" when I sent word your way!
But your mind you closed, refusing to open your hearts door.
Now you are lost, because you did not want to learn anymore.

One must shift his actions, as he learns the new that comes to light.
For God is always revealing His will, and showing what is right.
Life is a continual process, of growing in knowledge and truth.
Not one of being surrounded, and incased in a none learning booth.
Growth occurs when a yearning exist, to place knowledge in store.
And no longer will be the thoughts, "I don't want to learn anymore!"

# Identity Theft

The little girl was pulled from the lake one dreary day.
No identification was found at the place where she lay.
A call went out to cities and towns all around.
Yet no identity for the little girl was ever found.
No one responded to the calls that were made.
Therefore in a grave Little Jane doe was laid.
Jane Doe! A name that's common for the unknown.
But who is she really? For her identity was gone.
Lying in the ground with her name taken away.
The world doesn't know her, and lost she will stay.
Because without a name, so that all will know!
One falls in the ranks of John or Jane Doe.
Standing all alone for the whole world to see.
Imagine how you would feel without an identity?
How would you feel if no one spoke your name?
And referred to you and others with the same?
If Jane Doe was the name that was applied to all.
How would you know when your name was called?
For one to respond on the name you rely.
To the one you speak, you must identify.
Take away a name and you have won the war.
For it's sure no one will ever know who you are.
Take away the name, if that's really your goal.
And the individual will be left no longer whole.
Take away a name! What is it that's left?
It's a true victim of identity theft!
How could you find this one you seek?
When there is nothing to look for that is unique.
Such is one who's recorded in Gods word.
And yet, a name most have never heard.

In His word it is mentioned again and again.
That He desired his name be known amongst men.
Thou shall not steal! The Scriptures clearly say.
Yet Satan. Through Man. is trying to take it away.
And Satan has confused him into believing a lie.
In the same way he caused Adam and eve to die.
Many people are beguiled and simply do not know.
God's identity has been replaced with a name like Jane Doe.
A common name that is now spoken free.
And places the Creator with other deities.
Satan is trying to leave nothing of it left.
Therefore he is guilty of Identity Theft.
Something to ponder as you move through the day.
There is a need to find His name and without delay.

# If there were no rules

How would you feel having a car with no rules on how to start?
Or playing a game and of the rules one would have no part.

How would you feel driving on a street without stop signs?
How about on the hi-way with no dividing lines?

How would you feel living in a family with children who will not obey?
Or in a town that allowed everyone to have their own way.

How about a society with rights to do their own thing?
Can we imagine the trouble bringing all the sorrow and pain?

No society can survive, without a means of control.
It is easy to see by looking at the sad stories unfold.

To show love is to obey our parents, and the laws of the land.
Yah, our Creator is no different with respect to His plan.

He knew we could not survive, without laws for a helping hand.
But the desire to put them aside, is in the mind of man.

It appears all laws except the Sabbath, are found to be okay.
But this law seems to always get in the way.

If it could be erased it would make things so good.
Then man could really be free to do as he would.

All kinds of excuses have moved to erase the thought.
And he is working hard to bring this day to a halt.

But this must be said, concerning what we know is true.
We can't show Him love, without being willing to obey His rule.

# In Human Hands

As human hands reach to give a start in life's
long journey that wonders through the sky.
The Creators hands reach down for each person
To offer help when they cry.
So look up to the heavens, and the sky that's blue.
And wait for Gods hand to reach down for you.

# In search of a rare Christian

I started a journey today to find an obedient Christian.
I know I have passed one now and then.
I felt I could find someone who really would stand out.
Surely there are a few and this I have no doubt.
How will I know the one that is really real?
Can I tell by looking? Or must there be a seal?
To one I came and ask to please identify.
And to me, he said Gods word he would not deny.
To another I ask, are you sir, really living right?
"Yes!" he said to me, I too have the light!
But much to my dismay while my search was on.
I could not find anyone that stood out alone.
For all that I asked surely claimed to be true.
But they did the same as others claiming new.
My search led me over the sea and across the land.
I found no difference when they gave a helping hand.
Somewhere in this world there surely has to be.
One that really is different will be shown to me.
There has to be something for surely all are not the same.
Though they all proclaim to know and use Jesus' name
Each claim to know and love all the values of life.
And all are faced with envy, sorrow and strife.
They feel actions are important to serve as a mark.
All feel they emptied their sins and made a new start.
Something really different is a hard thing to see.
For all acted and looked alike, but I know here has to be.
Then I observed someone who forfeited all things of his heart.
For there was something in which he choose never to have a part.
For upon the Sabbath  he was required to break.
Or forfeit his things in life to obtain a heavenly stake.

Now this is something that one is rarely going to see.
For someone to loose all in order to be free.
This one thing I surely to you will gladly tell.
To really obey the Creators laws is for one to do well.
It is not all one has to do to stand out from amongst the rest.
But those who obey the Lord are the ones that pass the test.
My search is over I have found the thing that stands out.
The identity lies in the Sabbath, and to that there is no doubt.

# In the days of old

Adam and Eve were created in the days of old.
Noah and his family, remember how that story is told!
How Abraham, traveled looking for the Promised Land.
Remember how David, slew the Giant with his hand?
And Joseph, while in Egypt, was a leader in his day.
Solomon, A man of wisdom, left words for life's new way.
You have heard about Jericho as Joshua walked around.
How the people blew trumpets and the walls tumbled down.
Then there was John the Baptist, preaching about the end.
Sayings "repent" and be baptized, and wash away your sins!
All these stories of old, I know you have heard!
Even the latest one of Gods Son called "The Word"
How He left instructions for man to follow through.
In order to prove to God our love was really true.
These stories have a meaning that is very dear.
They are for our learning and to bring us very near.
Every story that is told, is there for a cause.
They were examples to see if man would rise or fall.
The greatest example is by the brother we know.
The Resurrected one that sets our hearts aglow.
His example is one that requires a lot of toil and strife.
Yet, has a reward for overcoming, and that's eternal life.

# Insurance

If you were getting on an airplane and another passenger made the statement
"This thing may crash!" What would you do?
Would your reaction be different if that person were dressed in a mechanics suit?
And what if you were flying along and that mechanic made the statement
and you looked out the window and saw an object loose and flapping on
the wing. How much different would your thoughts be now? It is really
against human nature to think something is going to happen to them that
involves death. Unless they can see the proof it is always felt it will happen
to the other person.

If a person told one of us we were going to die, How would we feel?
Would we not have a little doubt? What if that person were a doctor?
Would we still have the same kind of doubt? And what if that doctor
showed us the proof? How much of that little doubt would be changed to
real concern?
Would we not be about our business trying to get everything straight?
We see people all around us dying every day and yet we still carry enough
doubt to think "It won't happen to us. It's the other guy" We are told
we are going to die and that it could occur at any moment. We see it all
around and yet there remains a doubt that it will really occur to anyone of
us. We have more faith in the fact someone will steal our car, break into
our house, or that we will be in an auto accident than we have in the fact
we could die at any moment? Yet, we buy many kinds of insurance policies.
Think about it! We buy insurance on our house,
Jewelry, cars, and all matter of other things. All the insurance we purchase is
to benefit ourselves in case of **loss**. We do buy life insurance but who will
that benefit? What most forget to buy is the real "Life insurance policy"
Life insurance that has a pay back in real value, not money but "Real Life"
Why do people choose not to invest into this "Real Life" insurance?

42

It's because we reach to hold on to the things we can see. We see auto crashes, houses burn, and people dying, but we have never seen what happens after death.

And because we can't see it, we have that little doubt as to it happening. We seem to just blot it out. That "Real Life" insurance that has a pay back of "Real Life" can be purchased for a premium **while** we are still alive and well. Matter of fact that's when it has to be purchased. We can't wait until the plane has took off to buy it either. The premium sometimes becomes hard to pay for it could amount to value for value in some cases. The premium is not paid with money. It is paid with actions! Actions of faith and actions of deeds. Not any one of the two alone but both together, they can not be separated. Faith in believing and Actions of obedience. Faith only is one half of the payment and obedience only is the other half. Faith and obedience both make up the full policy payment program and the pay back of this policy has a one time pay back that is eternal with the issuer of insurance.

# Is your Spirit Well?

A question that is asked from time, to time.
Done in an attempt to bring peace of mind.
But peace is hard to come by in a world that binds.
For carnal is the nature that usually shines.
From the garden in Eden comes the story to tell.
Along  with the question "Is your Spirit well?"
Trouble has followed mankind from then until now.
Man trying to guide himself, yet not knowing how.
Rejecting the advice given to help along the way.
And trying to make things happen each and every day.
The nature of man is to guide his life and have his own way.
While refusing to allow his maker to have a say.
And when the night comes and the body is frail.
Comes again the question, "Is your Spirit well?"
While the body is fatigued and fading away.
Man pushes himself to make it another day.
His physical ailments are always on his mind.
As he calls for healing from the Creator of mankind.
Yet, when his body is down and fading every day.
And he sees his spirit ready to be on its way.
He looks at himself, for only he can tell.
And ask the question, "Is my spirit well? "
Is your Spirit well?   Or is it sad and blue?
For it is a reflection of the really you.
Is my spirit well? A question everyone must ask.
For it must be in order for death to pass.
The body can wilt and eventually fall.
But the Spirit must be well through it all.
For it's the spirit of Yah that is loaned to us.
Until the day we return to the dust.
So check yourself for only you can tell.
And ask yourself the question, "Is my spirit well? "

# It's Hard to Imagine

It's hard to imagine the beauty man has been introduced to.
Or what he may see during the life he goes through.
It's hard to imagine how the wings of a bird move up and down.
Or why the kangaroo and locust spend their life jumping around.
It's hard to imagine how the waters that slowly fall.
Can so swiftly move across the ground.
To become so calm and peaceful as it simply lays around.
It's hard to imagine how the wind as a gentle breeze.
That slowly moves across your face.
Can suddenly change to a violent storm to roar at a rapid pace.
It's hard to imagine, how fire can destroy all that one has known.
And yet, save the life of a body that's chilled to the bone.
It's hard to imagine the snow in a blizzard furry.
Can smother under its cover so white.
And yet, become a blanket of wonder and a child's greatest delight.
It's hard to imagine how the lighting bolt with its brightness in the night.
Can shatter the largest tree with the impact of its might.
It's hard to imagine the vast space that's in the sky above.
Or to imagine the emptiness of the heart that has no love.
It's hard to imagine why things gentle and strong were given to man.
Or how it's possible to have a Creator that's willing to hold his hand.
It's hard to imagine a gift so great as the gift of eternal life.
Or how one can live forever, in a life without toil and strife.
Yes, it's hard to imagine all these things that I have listed above.
But most of all, it's hardest to imagine, Gods greatest gift of LOVE

# Just how close are we, Lord?

In serious reverence we ask you to bless our food to the nourishment of our bodies. But after we have eaten our fill, we throw the sometimes heaping left over's into the trash cans to be carried to the city dumps. Many times we pile our plates full only to eat small amounts and then allow the rest to be thrown away. We even give to our children amounts that they can not eat or do not want. And then teach them it is not necessary to eat it all. We tell them they should not be wasteful. However they are not really disciplined into learning the reality. Therefore they too will not require their children not to waste. Thus the loss of value is passed to the next generation. It appears we have become as those we complain about in our aid programs from the government. Those that seek aid and yet do not appear to appreciate it by their demonstration of wastefulness. Doesn't it show they do not really appreciate what has been given to them? Could the Creator be looking at us in the same way? We are quick to remember the need for water, electricity, and other things we have become accustomed to in a time of crisis. However, as soon as the crisis has passed an the items are restored we just as quickly loose their value. While they were lost, we found we could do many things with just a small amount of each. However, it appears that as soon as we have them back we once again start using the many times more than necessary. Not only are we wasteful in these things, we are in other areas as well. We give so many toys to children with no responsibility attached to them. They are scattered about the yard and allowed to ruin. And once again this teaching is passed on to the next generation. The Creator has been good to us. Maybe too good. It appears we may have truly lost the value of your creations and this brings about a question. Could we be praying in vain when we ask you to bless our food? Or thank you for what we have and yet truly make no move to preserve it? It may well be known we can not feed the world nor be required by you to do so. Nor that we should do without your blessings. But do you require us to use what you give us with appreciation? Did you give all this to us so we may loose our respect for it?  Could the way we handle all our blessing be another test of stewardship that we will be judged in?  Father, would you allow your Holy Spirit to impress upon our minds these questions when we cook, buy, and in other ways use what you have given us?  Are we close to making a Mockery of ourselves?  Impress upon us how you would view our activities.  Do you smile down on us, knowing we thank you without truly demonstrating a desire nor real efforts to use your creation sparingly?  Just how close are we to being cast aside and all the abundance of material things taken away?

Just how close are we Lord?

# Justify

Life is full of actions we must take along the way.
Some made hastily without considering what others have to say.

We can guide our path and on others we do not have to rely.
All things can be considered right, if we want to justify.

We can shun our neighbor, causing hurt and call it satisfaction.
And if we want we can find a way to justify that kind of action.

Thoughts of the golden rule, can be left sitting by the way.
If we desire it we can justify anything we say.

Hurting words destroying the feelings found deep inside.
Can be called "right," and in our minds be justified.


To steel from another, we can find reasons for that too.
All we have to do is justify a reason to break that golden rule.

To get out of responsibilities and to place them upon another's back.
Is not a problem at all, when it comes to justifying our slack.

To raise our nose at the one whose life does not meet our wants.
Is another task easy to justify with the right choice of don'ts.

Yes. We can do anything we wish and consider ourselves right,
If we simply look at the excuses placed in our sight.

But one thing generally forgotten, when we justify our ways.
There is certain to be a time for justification to the Ancient of days.

When we break His laws and try to justify our intent.
We will find He has a rule that justification was not meant.

His commands are plain and no manner of excuses will do.
They are given as directives, that everyone must be true.

If we control our thoughts to bring ourselves completely in line.
We will not have to justify our actions each and every time.

And when we stand in front of the King, as our past is shown that day.
We will not be looking for a way to justify what we say.

# Knowing Satan

Satan is the angel of the night – he is not a guiding light.
Then said Jesus to Satan! Get away from me! For it is written that one shall
worship the Lord your God and Him only shall you serve. And at another time
Jesus turned to Peter and said "Get behind me Satan".
Because you are an offense to me. You do not understand the things of god
but only the Understandings of men. For when the seed is sown, Satan goes
immediately and takes the word away that has been sown in their hearts. At
one time the Lord had to say to a man named Simon that Satan desired to
have him. That Satan would like to sift him as one would wheat. Oh yes!
Jesus is constantly asking for his people to open their eyes and turn from the
darkness unto the light.
To turn from the power of Satan and look to God.
To do this so they can receive forgiveness of their sins, and obtain an inheritance
amongst those that are sat apart by faith in Him.
Satan is vicious but his end is for sure. We are promised that the God of peace
will bruise Satan under his feet before long. But in the mean time we must be
careful to keep Satan from getting the advantage of us. Therefore we can't be
ignorant of his devices. For he is able to transform himself into even an angel of
light. We must be able to see that happening!   We must look for things like
powerful signs and lying wonders that are products of Satan himself. We must
be careful of his trickery because some have already turned aside and are
following him. Yes we must be careful of different doctrines because many do
not know the depths that Satan will go to trick people. But all is not lost for
us, because someday that old serpent called the Devil or Satan whose trickery
has traveled through out the whole world is going to be done away with. Yes
he and his angels are going to have their abilities taken away. They are going
to be bound for a thousand years and then we will have peace. But in the
mean time we must know how he works in order to avoid being tricked into
believing a lie, as Eve was and many on earth today.

# Letter to the Father

Dear Father:

How are things today? Sure hope they are going great! As for myself, I have a real problem that I need to discuss with you. I am confused about something in the world amongst your children. Everyone has an opinion on how you feel about the difference between the Sabbath and the first day of the week. . You know my record of the past! How I worshipped you on the first day of the week and how I understood you to tell me to start obeying the ten commandment laws. But Father, there are many different thoughts on your method of determining who, or who is not, going to obtain eternal life. I was in a conversation with friends when a person said there were Christians in all kinds of Sunday churches. Is this true Lord? Are there Christians you are going to give eternal life too in these churches? ( sure would be happy if that was true, for many are my friends and their worship is very sincere. I was told by some that observe the first day that You came down and heal the sick and do all kinds of good things, for them. This is ready confusing and I don't understand.   However, if this is true, could I ask why you had me move from the church I was in to one that honors Your Sabbath?   I know people get well after prayer but please tell me why you would go into their mist and grant their prayers when they do not obey your laws? I know if they are getting well after prayer that someone must be doing it.   If you are in their mist doing all kinds of good, then it really makes it harder for me to understand why you had me move from the Sunday keeping church. I was worshipping you while I was a member of that church, wasn't I?   I was doing everything I could for you, wasn't I? And it was much easier while I was in that church. I could honor your birth during Christmas time and celebrate along with all the others that exchanged gifts and had a lot of fun.  I would not have to suffer the hardship I have to go through with my family and my friends concerning this holiday.  I could also worship you at Easter and be with, and enjoy my children and friends and hunt Easter eggs that represent you in the God head. After all! was that not teaching them about You? And there were no problems at work while I was serving you on Sunday! And I could work all the time as long as I went to church for worship service to You. Father! I have always given you the credit for things I do and especially for my job. It has allowed me to raise my family without worry and make enough money to help support the church. I know you remember when I first got the call to go to work there? I thanked you constantly for that day! I remember it so well. How I felt You were granting me the job because I had worked hard in trying to serve You in the church. Now I may have to give up all that! and I would gladly do so if You thought it was really necessary. But I really don't understand why it should be if You find favor with those not honoring the Sabbath, If it was okay to worship You on the first day of the week, and my actions were good, then I have got to ask you again, why did You ask me to move to the Sabbath? That is surely not like You! Why would You ask me to move from a place that I felt You would automatically give me eternal life just for believing on You and put me in a place You knew I could loose all that I had because the others feel strongly against the belief in the Sabbath. I could even fail in my efforts and loose my eternal chance with you. If you do not place a difference between those who do, and do not follow your laws. Then I ask You to allow me to go back to worshipping You on Sunday. It was so much easier to serve You then. Nobody found fault with me because I could go along with the traditions of man that have been converted into worshipping You. All we had to do was give them a religious meaning and apply them to You. Wasn't that okay? And I would not be so easy to spot either. My being and doing the same things as everyone else around me. And I could eat anything I wanted and even work all the time. I would blend in with the majority of people. If I could do that then it would not cause any problems for me in trying to honor the Sabbath. Because I could help them out at work. All they ask is that I work when they need me. Isn't that in the area of "doing good"? if they are right when they say You will grant the same gift to those who do not struggle to obey Your laws as to those who do. Then maybe they will have the same chance as I do. But if that really is the case, then You have to please tell me! Could there be a different standard that allows You to give life to the one obeying Your laws and also to the one that does not obey them? If there is a different standard then it really does cause me confusion. Surely Your being the same yesterday, today, and forever will not allow You to refuse eternal life to those who (did not) keep your Sabbath in the old days, and then give it to those (who do not) keep it in this day and time. Surely I can depend on Your not doing a flip-flop in your directives! Surely we can depend on that) I really hope You do not feel my questions are out of line, for we could sure use some straightening out in our thinking down here. Father, I really do need Your help in understanding this thing. Please deliver Your answer as quick as You can. And thanks for your patience.

# "Life can be so hard"

Life can be so hard.
From the trials we're put though.
We strive to do the best we can.
In all the things we do.

But then we hit a stumbling block.
And on our knees we fall.
To ask our heavenly Father.
To help us through it all.

It's hard to take when people judge you.
When they've not been in your place.
Know matter what they say or feel.
Your saved alone through Gods own grace.

So when we're up and on our feet.
We turn to him and say.
I thank you Lord for a battle won.
And a start of a brand new day.

So life can be so hard at times.
From the things that we're put though.
But knowing God is number one.
He will always help me and you.

By Laura Turner
(Printed by permission)

# Little Wrongs are Important

Just driving along with the greatest of ease,
Sixty five in a fifty five, enjoying the breeze.
The train was approaching to the crossing very near.
I'll wait until it's very close, "I have no fear!"
I saw the stop sign, and to a slow speed I came.
For stop to me, does not always mean the same.
Nothing wrong with a little trick now and then.
After all! I consider the train driver to be my friend.
I listened intently to the words of the joke.
Vulgar now and then but I felt they would not provoke.
I said "Oh Friend" have you heard the word."
Just a little rumor I recently heard.
My brother did wrong and I told it to a friend.
Better to share it with another than to suppress it within.
I watched the neighbor and I know he needed help.
But I didn't have the time, and this is how I felt.
My boss ask me why I did it, and I didn't tell him all.
No need to be so accurate, for he will not recall.
One little bolt was all I needed to take from the bin.
I know it won't be missed and I don't plan to do it again.
Just to write a line or two and three pages is all I need.
I'll just take 6 and later write something else to read.
Can't the character of Christ be displayed to the others we know?
While breaking the laws a little, for it will never show.
We have the blood of Christ to cover these little things we've done!
No need to change, for it won't take away what we've won.
The question posed for thought to consider today,
Do we have to remove the little wrongs, in order to change our way?
When Christ comes again and we face Him one on one,
Will He say "you did your best, eternal life you've won?"
Or will you stand in awe as He says the words to thee.
Little wrongs were important and you chose not to see.

# Lonely

Have you ever been lonely, sad and blue?
Wishing for a friend you could know was true.

Have you ever been lost in a forest at night?
Not knowing how to turn with the absence of light.

Have you ever been afraid of objects not seen?
Not knowing of strength and no place to lean.

Have you ever been on top of a mountain high?
And were so afraid that you were going to die.

Have you ever wished for someone near?
To have and to hold to remove all fear.

There is someone with a joy to reveal.
That will remove the sadness making life so real.

Where is this one that can be made known?
That will remove these things and not leave us alone.

Have you ever looked closely at a flowers glow?
That's the Creator letting His colors show.

Have you really looked at the sky so blue?
And seen the beauty He is showing to you.
This line is not double spaced as the others.
It's His carpet that makes such a pretty scene.

Have you taken the time to walk in the valley low?
To feel the creation of Yah, He's trying to show.

Have you gazed at the light of a distant star?
And wondered if that is where the angels are.

Have you stopped and thought so you could know?
We can put away loneliness and God's love will show.

For if in everything we see, we will look for Him.
We will always find Him, again and again.

Loneliness is not a state of mind or a trend.
For in every place we look we can find this friend.

# Lost

I have a little something I would like to talk about.
We used to have a lot of it to make us jump and shout.
It was something we had to work on, in order for it to build.
It was something that got bigger, as we saw the things so real.
We used to carry it with us, as we went to and fro.
Now we don't have as much of it, to take wherever we go.
Somehow we have lost a lot of the full cup we once had.
Or maybe we have only half of it, and that makes me very sad.
Seems like we loose more and more ,as on a human we depend.
I'm afraid if we are not careful, we will loose it in the end.
This thing I speak of is most important of all I know.
For without it, to be with the Lord we can never go.
We are told to keep it, and always have it near.
And I know, without it, I would always be lost in fear.
Somehow we must gain back, that which we have lost.
It will take a lot of exercise, but we must be willing to pay the cost.
For without it we can never stand, at the Saviors door.
Yes, without our Faith, we will be lost forever more.

# Love

Love is a word for you and me As you read this you will see!

L. is for life together always to be!

O. is for onward until death takes us away.

V. is for victory of overcoming on resurrection day.

E. is forever we will spend, eternity together again.

# Map Route

There were two sons who lived in a city on the East coast. While making a move to California their father told them that if they would live a good life, do what was right, love him, honor him, obey him, and tell people the good things he had done. He would give each one of them a reward of one million dollars. All they had to do was follow his map to San Francisco. He gave instructions on what route to take. This is what he told them to do. Take route eighty to interstate forty. Take forty to Barstow. Then take highway fifty eight to Bakersfield until you come to highway five, Then take five to five eighty and five eighty to San Francisco. This is the way I have mapped out and this is the way you are to go. While traveling one noticed that route ninety nine went alone side of highway five to five eighty. It did not appear to have the ups and downs the other route had going over the mountains. There was no difference in miles and the traffic also appeared less hazardous. He started to thinking about the ease of travel and to himself said. My father wanted us to take the best route to San Francisco and it appears this is really the best way. After all, surely he did not care if we made a decision on our own and changed the instructions a little bit. It looks like I will have to go over a lot of hills and valleys using his map. It surely would be okay to detour for the sake of making it a little easier to get there! After all, is not the end result the important thing? After considerable thought he justified his reasoning and took the route of his choice. Both sons arrived at the same time and at the same place. Both had taken the route they felt was the best. Both felt they had earned the reward. Both had honored him, built him up, told people about him, loved him, traveled from New York to San Francisco as requested. Took the "best" route. Arrived at the same place at the same time with great joy on their faces.

**Shall they both receive the same reward?**

# My Past

Guess what my friend, what has happened to me?
I have just been told how I came to be!
They have figured it out from evidence found.
Our ancestral links are found in the ground.
They have dug them up part by part.
Assembled them together and applied the art.
But, low and behold guess what I have found?
They haven't found much buried way down.
All the parts found from then until today.
Really just prove creation was the way.
Just a simple search and you will see.
That creation is what caused you and me.

# Opinions

Confusion exist in our churches today.
For opinions abound that determine a say.
Feelings containing many thoughts of doubt.
Teachings varying from sincere actions to a shout.
Traditions held from many years ago.
To the present generation of feelings that flow.
The anchor slips from time to time, it appears to me
Forming a belief not intended to be.
The foundation that once was taught has come to past.
New teachings have eroded bringing questions to ask.
Thoughts of love are clouded to me it does appear.
Concern for self are desires wanted near.
Your opinion is important one will say to a friend.
My opinion is also a factor to be repeated again and again.
You teach this, I believe that, it is the feeling that counts.
It is the importance of a subject that in time will amount.
The need to follow a set rule is slowly being erased.
I can do as desired, letting my conscience set the pace.
Yes, this is the way to live, with no trouble for a task.
Life is made simple and being ridged has become the past.
As time has passed from the beginning until today.
The commandments of God and Christ are now easier to obey.
What is now wrong for me may be right for you.
Each to understand the meanings of how we are to be true.
As time continues the meanings will change again.
Until the lost are confused and no one will win.
Beware of the traditions of man! See words to guide us right.
Found in the instructions of God to lead us to eternal light.
These words were put forth in hope to provoke a thought.
We need to know what Gods word has really taught.

# Our plates are full

We thank the Lord for the food we eat.
He has given so much it falls to our feet.

We thank Him for our food each day.
Yet eat only part and allow the rest to lay.

We thank Him much for the blessings He gave.
While throwing some away for the sweets we crave.

Our plates are full of the bountiful treat.
For He has blessed us with so much to eat.

We open the cans and heap in a pile.
While taking on excess and walk with a smile.

What's left on our plate goes in a garbage can.
Without thought for another hungry man.

Our excess has made room for greed.
Because we take it without true need.

The food that is left and chosen not to eat,
Is enough to be a hungry man's treat.

We can gorge ourselves all day long.
Yet never see our wastefulness as anything wrong.

Bless this food to the Lord we pray.
Never giving thought to what we throw away.

The animals of God never see our waste.
For we put it in sacks and never leave a trace.

It should make one wonder if God looks with a smile.
When watching us throw His food in a pile.

It's all for ourselves and no one need to share.
Should bring a concern about Satan's snare.

How would we feel if we gave of ourselves?
Just to watch one waste what they took from the shelves.

How long would we continue to give each day?
While watching Our food be thrown away?

Let us consider God's grocery store.
And vow not to waste our food anymore.

And if we have more than we can use.
Let's find a way not to abuse.

For God is generous in His gift to us.
Therefore, remember it's in God we trust.

# Pain

He awakes today, the morning light to see.
He is filled to the fullest with complete animosity.

He feels the pain and agony while moving around.
It clouds his mind with doubts and holds his spirit down.

He falls backward each time he faces the day.
Trying to build the belief that it will go away.

The heart aches continue with each pain and woe.
As another shocking story he has to be told.

There comes a time when he is deep in despair.
Can't find room within himself for love to share.

As each day is ending and the night comes along.
He finds himself empty and all alone.

Always searching for help within his misery.
Yet crushed within for everyone to see.

His thoughts are to completely pull inside.
By doing so the sadness he can hide.

As he sets looking within himself.
He encloses all the love he has left.

Pulling all his feelings from around and about.
Shutting in all that surrounds him and locking it out.

It seems there is no use to try and go on.
All the hope he had now seems to be gone.

He feels forsaken by the one above.
Because he is not able to see his love.

Why, he ask! has the maker forgotten me?
As the thought rushes by, "Today I can see!"

His love for me is supposed to always be near!
At that time he remembers he can still hear.

But when I walk I should not stumble and fall.
Thoughts go through his mind of one that can't walk at all.

Why all the pain? The reason he can not see,
As he is reminded of the lonely one with leprosy.

He should be happy and full of joy and cheer.
As he looks upon his children who hold him so dear.

If only he could, some of these trials win!
As he grasps the hand of the wife who has stood by him.

As he looks around in his deep despair.
If he would only open his eyes, he would see those who really care.

For in his thoughts of misery he has a lot to see.
Having things that for others it was not meant to be.

He has, his sight, hearing ,his wife, and children of love.
He should see that  he is really blessed by the one from above.

Shall he lock away the gift he also can give?
Or shall he take one day at a time and with that live?

Let him use what he has to show and receive love.
The greatest gift bestowed on man from above.

For man is but a whisper while passing through this life.
Always fighting the whims, woes, toils and strife.

It is better to have lived a few days standing tall.
Than never have the joy of life and love at all.

# Pastor appreciation

Around the nation in a very special way.
People are observing Pastor Appreciation day.
A day set aside to share in the story.
Of how throughout the year they have shown God's glory.
They study hard and burn the midnight oil.
Just to plant a few seeds in our human soil
Just a short time to speak for the Creator above.
To lead the church with heartfelt love.
30 minutes or maybe an hour once in a while.
To try and make a point to those in the wild.
One may not come when they have finished the speech.
Yet because of love they continue to preach.
Their faith is in God and is hoped not to cease.
Always believing that He will give an increase.
And as one passes when the service is through.
Reaching for their hand is the golden rule.
The leader of a flock they have chosen to be.
And twenty four hours a day will oversee.
Though many may view the job as an easy task.
They would turn it down should anyone ask.
Many disappointments are faced from day to day.
Yet, they care for each member in a special way.
The desire to see us bond as we go along.
They say in a prayer before the day is gone.
With all these thoughts that have come to mind.
The evidence is clear that they are one of a kind.
Pastor appreciation day only comes once a year.
To bring us together to share what is dear.
Though it's true all year long and yet we rarely say.
**Pastor,** we choose to confirm that we love you on this
Pastor appreciation day.

# Pick and Choose

In the beginning instructions were laid down.
Direct were the points, there was no fooling around.
No negotiation with God on the directives given.
If one chose not to follow, he would not continue living.
Christ came along and continued this trend.
Explaining that not obeying meant death at the end.
The choice was clear until man chose to say.
Things are not the same because Christ changed the day.
And from that action man started toward the fall.
Church after church was formed that now affects us all.
There are so many that teach what they want.
And today what was "do" has now become "don't".
And should one's feelings, convince them that something is right.
They can choose a teaching to place them in the light.
And if one chooses to do, what God stated is wrong.
They to can choose a group  teaching it's all right to go along.
So as one can see, we have a list to choose from.
We can pick and choose them all or just one.
We can also go to one church today and another one tomorrow.
In this we can satisfy ourselves by removing all of our sorrow.
But the truth that exist for man today.
Is to pick and choose only what the Creator had to say.
So as one ponders the thoughts and decisions to make.
Remember to only pick and choose Gods directions to avoid
the mistake.

# Quick sand

As I look back to the days of old,
Recalling worldly desires I tried to hold.
All things I did, I did by myself.
I determined my destiny, by the way I felt.
I needed no other to guide my way.
For I had the knowledge of events for the day.
One day I slipped, and into a pit I fell.
No problem, I thought, I can get out of the well!
So I reached for a tree limb, to get a hold.
I felt no fear for I was very bold.
I reached for the branch as I was sinking.
Yet, no fear was felt! That's what I was thinking.
When pulling on the limb, to get myself out.
I was going to make it, there was no doubt.
But the limb broke, with a loud crack.
And filled me with concern, as I slipped back.
A plea for help was my desire to say.
Just a helping hand from the world on their way.
As I looked around to see many there.
Yet, to pull me from the quicksand they wouldn't dare.
I knew I was in trouble, as I was sinking low.
Surely there is someone, to help me I know.
Now to my waist and slowly sinking down.
Fear came over me, as I looked around.
For the pit was full of those who had fell in.
And one could not tell how long they had been.
As the world stood around, and were looking at me.
I could see no help was going to come to be.
They did not wish to lend a helping hand.
Because they too were standing in the quicksand.

Up to my neck, the sand had now come.
My mind flashed back to past thoughts so dumb.
For thinking to myself, that I could always stand.
Never did I think I would need a helping hand.
But to my surprise, I have found myself here.
And in my despair, I realized the fear.
The fear that my life was coming to an end.
While finding myself in this pit of sin.
Darkness starts to come, as I'm slipping in.
Then I see a light shining amongst men.
I beg for the light to take the darkness away.
And grant me life for another day.
I reached up my hand toward the light.
Asking, please don't let me fall into the night.
Suddenly I felt myself being lifted high.
By a hand that came down from the sky.
It pulled me out from where I had been.
It was the light that is shown among men.
It was the light of life that's given free.
And that light had just rescued me.
No longer can I say, I will do it alone.
For I must have help from the one on the throne.

# Relaxing

In a rocking chair I sat, relaxing on a porch of old.
Reminiscing of my youth and of the stories told.
Gazing into the night at the stars so bright.
Watching and wondering, seeing the Creators Delight.
I envisioned the beauty as a child would a toy.
Imagining the thoughts of God making things to enjoy.
Beautiful! He surely said, as the finishing touch was made.
He completed His task, only one more foundation to be laid.
I've made everything except an image to represent me.
The only task left is to make man for my creations to see.
A master plan I have that require many test to prove a point.
Sadness and anger must past before long life I will appoint.
Yes, there is beauty in the stars and the clear blue sky.
But the wonder of my creation is man, this I will not deny.
This will be my master piece for me to show my love.
Unique in the universe, this final creation from above.
I will give to him rule over all the things I've made.
He can decide for himself the foundation I've already laid.
Through him I will show a love that is forever high.
It will require a sacrifice on which he can rely.
A devotion to human kind in the greatest form of love.
A special showing of care that none could be above.
A Love that grants to another all joys he can see.
The only thing I will ask is obedience be returned to me.
Obedience toward his creator is not to great to ask.
And for this devotion to me, I give him a life to last.
For I know he truly loves me if through my only Son.
He does what is necessary to see that my task are done.

# Religious division

We read a book and tell the story of a man that did good deeds,
He told us the way and things to do, and then he said "take heed"
"One can live forever" He said, if you will only believe in me.
But many you know, read what He told, but still will not see.
With the examples of righteousness He has paved the way.
For those who believe and obey, to have eternal life one day
But those who did not like His way, hung him to a tree.
Righteous He was, in dying He said, "Forgive them that do this to me."
The story has been told many ways I know, from then until today.
Told by few, changed by many, until most do not know the way.
The Bible through rain and snow, came down all these years.
People cried, many died, while shielding it with their tears.
Men come, and men read, and then they make a creed.
Changing this, while saying that, all because of greed.
They have formed many religions in this world today.
And not two of them have the same thing to say!
One says this! One says that! Another says yes or no!
Another doesn't know where he is at, nor where to go!
Religious Division! Surely we know it's not right!
The Savior told only one story that leads to eternal light.
I ask many, how do you understand all of these things?
They say their part, different though, but all in Jesus' name.
One says this! and another that, and none speak the same.
Indeed I ask, by what authority are they using His name?
Oh I wonder and how I pray, that all will be one way.
That we can talk and understand together someday.
When we stand in front of the Savior He may say with a shout!
My word was there, simple and fair, but you were running about!
Some of you took me seriously and believed in my way.
So come to me! Look and see, have eternal life today!
There is a warning in these words you have just read.
Leave out Traditions, and opinion, when reading what He said.
To make sure you are on the way that leads to eternal light.
For it's sad you know! But many have chosen, the way to eternal night.

# Satan's Playground

It is the devils desire to trod amongst the best.
And place before them a failing test.

His eye falls upon those striving to be true.
With hopes of destroying both me and you!

And down into the mist he will cast his spell.
Disturbing the minds of those wanting to do well.

He throws an anchor into the mist of the crowd.
And starts the rumors by sighing loud.

First he signals an untruth from out of ones heart.
Smiling as he has managed to find his start.

Then slowly but surely he forms the plot.
Until there is deceit and discord, and he smiles a lot.

Soon strife and anger within a group will abound.
And Satan has found another playground.

Love is brought from real to make believe.
All because of his ability to deceive.

A church is torn apart with wounds very deep.
And Satan is relaxing in a slumbering sleep.

The love for a brother has drawn to a close.
Because to disobey the Creator is what has been chose.

How does one defeat the evil and bring him down.
And take away his ability to keep the playground?

Only by following the instructions of God above.
Will let all the actions be guided by love.

Then Satan will have no reason to hang around.
For it would be impossible to start his playground.

# Satan's World

Is this Satan's world? The question I ask you today.
Or is it just a place God's assigned him to stay?
Could he own the world and all the peoples will?
And God just own the cattle of a thousand hills.
Could the evil one make the sun and stars shine so bright?
Yet, work so hard to destroy both the day and night.
Could the god of this world bring peace to the heart?
If his real desire is to destroy every part.
Would the one who has caused man to fall.
Desire to guarantee the safety for one and all?
Can the beauty of the earth as seen from above.
Be credited to the one who really has no love?
Can the stars that shine throughout the night.
Shine as an emblem of Satan's delight?
Can the birds that fly from tree to tree.
Be a tribute to the evil one for the world to see?
Can the accumulation of love that dwells within.
Originate from the master of the original sin?
You can be assured from above without any doubt.
This father of lies really carries no clout.
But we had best get to know his devious ways.
Less he robs us of our inheritance from the ancient of days.

# Second Coming of Christ

I could not rest for I tossed and turned in my sleep.
Thinking of the 2nd coming and when I awake from the deep.
Watch for His coming and all the signs you will see.
A message from preachers telling when it will be.
Look toward the east, and you will see it start.
Signs in the heavens and the moon will turn dark.
Evidences will occur just before Christ comes home.
Eastern countries will gather never more to roam.
Wars, rumors of wars, just see what God will do.
Look into the future; see signs that mark what is true.
I found myself studying looking for what is shown,
For when I see the signs I won't be standing alone.
Watching and waiting getting ready to make haste.
Searching to find when the 2nd coming will take place.
Yes, we are busy looking for signs of his coming again.
Failing to concern ourselves with our present trend.
We may not understand what His words have really meant.
If we become so involved in looking for a future event.
When death occurs it's the 2nd coming that one will see.
And our state of being will determine what our future will be.
Our thoughts are always looking for the signs of tomorrow.
But if we are not ready for today, forever will be sorrow.
Therefore fix our eyes on actions at this present time.
And when we awake eternal life is what we will find

# Serve God, but what god do you serve?

Who is the Creator of the Universe? For it's plain to see.
There is some confusion as to how this came to be.
Many gods in this world are served by the people
Lords abound represented by some kind of steeple.
In Egypt it was Ra, the supreme god, and the cause of a creation story.
Phrased as lord and god of all and to him was given the glory.
In China there is another story on how all this came to be.
To Buddha were the honors given, as one bows for all to see.
The Greeks took no chance and left no one to wonder.
It was Thor they honored as the great god of thunder.
There was Estare, the love goddess of the past.
A name the tradition of Easter would make to last.
And Baal the sun god was called the supreme deity of all.
And today amongst many his name stands tall.
Glory and Praises were given to these gods of the past.
And today man still insures false gods will forever last.
For the days of our weeks are named after them.
And it keeps them alive again and again.

But amongst these gods and the stories told
Was the Unknown God of the days of old.
His name was given for the world to know.
But most have refused to let it show.
Many reasons are given from then until today.
As to why His name men will never say.
But recorded in his word is the evidence clear.
That man was to hold his name very dear.
It was to be known among all nations of men.
And to be called upon again and again.
It is the name that is silent in the world today.
And one that the people will rarely say.
There are many gods in the world it is taught.
But only one name has been brought to naught.
So, Identify the one on whom you call.
Thus removing any doubt from one and all.
Call him by name so that it is clear.
And the world will know what god you hold dear.
For without a name of which to identify.
There is no verification on whom you rely.

# Shall We Complain?

Shall I complain about the rain that washes the land away?
Shall I complain about snow that falls when desiring my way?
Shall I complain about the sun as its rays are beating down?
Or about the tornado when its winds blow my house down?
Shall I complain about the fire when my house it has burned?
Or continue to complain when I Have lost all that I've earned.
Shall I complain when for a reason I really feel left out?
Shall I complain when people show that in God they doubt?
Shall we complain when all our earthly friends are gone?
Shall we complain when people won't hear our song?

NO! We should not! Because
When it rains, it falls on all houses, whether brown or white.
The snow has no choice; it comes during the day or night.
The heat of the day will affect all men, both large and small.
And the cold of the world makes no choice; it affects us all.
All things that happen in nature affect everyone.
To some it's disliked; others, understood, what God has done.
Yes! it rains on the just and unjust - Both are treated alike.
It is the way they are received that counts in God's sight.
Both the right and wrong will suffer body deterioration.
Yet, the trip is made easier for some, because of a revelation.
All matter of trials and heartaches, we are able to overcome.
Because we have put our faith in the Creators Son.
Yes! The pain will be the same for one and all.
But, comfort will be to the one accepting the call.
For it is known that to obey God, there will be a cost.
But if we pay the price, Our life will not be lost.

# Snow on the Mountains

As the snow from the Creator covers the mountains so tall.
Offering a gift, and to everyone He sends the call.
He covers the sins of those who confess.
That His Son was showered with power from above.
And will grant them life forever,
Through His eternal love.

# Standing beside me

This friend of mine, That I hold dear.
Never have seen him, But I know he's near.
A book called the Bible, it tells me so.
I trust and believe, in this friend I know.

I'm on this earth, but it won't be long.
He has promised me life, after I 'm gone.
For this earthly life is only a flash.
Then I'll be with him forever at last.

This friend of mine, will be your friend too.
If you will trust in his golden rule.
Let him come in to your heart today.
Trust in his word and he will stay.

Oh what a wondrous time to spend.
Forever at last there is no end.
Then the reward of my faith I'll see.
Face to face with this friend I'll be.

Standing beside me, and beside me I see.
His image is there, walking with me.
Careful I'll walk and He will always be.
Standing beside, and walking with me.

# Storm Cloud

The power of a coming storm
that makes the thunder begin.
And the lightening bolt that strikes to
show the  power within.
Tis only a small example of the strength
the Eternal has shown to us.
The rest will be seen by those who in
God they trust.

# Strange Fire

There was a time in the days of old.
Moses, Aaron and his sons were told.

"Offer to Me a fire with incense".
But not a fire that wasn't meant.

From the thoughts of man the worship went.
The two offered a fire that God never sent.

So repelling it was, making Him mad.
That He took from them all they had.

So great a price the two had to pay.
When their only desire was to worship their way.

There must be a reason for what He did.
No mercy showed He, but took their lives instead.

Why was He so angry for the fire they sent?
Were they not worshipping the God Moses meant?

"It was a jealous God that led the people from bondage by night.
And the same God leads people today by the light.

To Him, if you worship, honor and obey.
You need to follow His instructions and not mans way.

For if you decide to offer Him your desire.
You will be in the place of offering a strange fire.

# Surely You Know!

When you are wondering in life without a place to go.
And you search for help, Tell me, Who do you know?

When you need someone to make the days sail by.
Who do you turn to, and on whom do you rely?

When trials are coming and you can't find your way.
Who do you turn to, at any hour of the day?

When you search to make luck evenly flow.
And you look for it everywhere, where do you go?

Do you seek a God that's made of wood or gold?
Or is it one that has come from the days of old?

Who is it that when for comfort you go?
Is it Ra, Baal, Zeus, or do you really know?

Do you find your comfort in a higher power?
Is it someone you can call on at any given hour?

Please tell me quickly so that I may go.
Just tell me his name, surely you know!

# Thanks

Please Yah! Let me thank you for my life this day.
Thank you for my eyes. To the see wonders of your way.

Thanks for the knowledge you are there to see.
Thanks for the special gift you gave to me.

Thank you for the beauty of life given for a while.
Thank you for the opportunity to become your child.

Thanks for the ability to someday see you.
And thanks for knowing you will see me through.

Thanks heavenly Father for the privilege to walk your land.
And thanks for the way you are willing to hold my hand.

Thanks for letting me know how all this came to be.
And thanks again Yahweh for your creating me.

Thanks for the feeling I get when I look at your stars.
Thank you for the desire to someday be where you are.

Thanks for the time you have given me to spend.
And thank you for the opportunity to live once again.

Thanks for a life with your wonders I am allowed to see.
Thank you once again for your creating me.

I know I've said thanks at the start of every phrase.
But for lack of a better word, Please except this praise.

# The "Ultimate" Love

Can we say, "I love you?" - Sure we can! We do it all the time! We say it to our wife, to our children, to our friends and we may even say it to a stranger. We emphasize it to our Christian brothers. - Love -- love -- love. We even sing a song, "Jesus loves me, this I know..." and "Oh how I love Jesus!" This word love is used over and over by, many of us. It is a part of our everyday speech. Much like the famous saying in the U.S. when we pass someone, we find ourselves saying, "How are you?" Or "How are you doing?" Just how much sincerity is in these questions? One way to find out is to stop the next person that says "how are you doing" and ask them if they have time to listen to your troubles. Don't be surprised if the answer is, "I don't have time!" It started off sincere but soon evolved into a simple saying with no real meaning. Is it possible that we can fall into the same rut? To arrive at the point of saying, "I love you! My brother or sister" and really not have that real feeling in it? Let's take a look at the various levels of the word "love". There appears to be several levels of meaning for this word. (Remember, I'm sharing thoughts; you may or may not agree but please think on them). First, there is the feeling of love one has for a stranger. Second is the feeling toward a friend. This feeling is a little different than the one for the stranger, is it not? Then we have the deeper loving feeling toward our off-spring, again different! (Could we not say most of us would do more for our children than for a friend or stranger? Now let's take the next step, "our mates" would it be incorrect to say most would abandon [all others] for their mates? This is the area (or level) we like to place our thoughts when we discuss "Love". But is it the level one feels toward anyone he/she meets? I think not! Let's take a close look at this deep feeling that one is supposed to have for the mate and the deep meaning of the statement Yahshua made when He said "No greater love can one show than to lay down his/her life for a friend". We have heard many statements such as, "He gave his life to rescue them!" or, "He gave his life for his friend!" and again, "I will do anything for you!"

# "It is hard to imagine a deeper love than this.

I would like to share thoughts of the feeling of love that is deeper than most think. It is called the "ultimate" love. We have heard this expression many times before. I believe it to be the highest feeling one can attain for his wife, child, friend, or even a stranger. You most probably have heard the statement, "No greater love hath any man than to lay down his life for a friend!" It was very hard for one to understand how it could be possible for a person to be killed while trying to rescue someone, or die in the line of duty and yet not have attained this "ultimate" love. After all, these had done what Christ said, Hadn't they? Yet, the question is asked. Did they perform the meaning of the love Christ spoke of? Did they truly lay down their life for a friend? Or did they die in the process of helping? The "Ultimate love - action Christ spoke of was one of Choice. Let me give this example. A person came upon a burning car and saw a person trapped inside. The person started towards the car in a move to rescue the trapped person. As he/she moves toward the vehicle a clear, firm, convincing voice is heard. "You are not coming back! If you go to rescue that person, you will be killed! He will be saved -but you are positively going to die!" What do you think would happen? How do you think he would react? If one can say with complete sincerity and without doubt, "I would lay down my life for you", "I would exchange my life so that you might live!" "I will die in your place if ever it becomes necessary!" then you will have attained that Ultimate love for another. You will have reached that level Christ spoke of when he said "Greater love hath no man than to lay down his life for a friend!" You see, he knew he was not coming back. He knew he was going to give his life so another might live. He willfully gave his life in exchange for his brothers, his sister, his friends, and even strangers. "He had this highest level of love". Some may feel bad if they think they do not have this feeling right now. Do not be dismayed for the possibility exist it may not show until a crisis time. And, if we do not practice the lesser levels that require sincere feelings toward all. (a forgiving nature, a willingness to gather towards our friends, our children, and even strangers. Will it be possible to perform the Ultimate, should it ever become necessary?

**That deep feeling of love that CHRIST felt for us all?**

# The Agony of the Worker

It's great being born in a country like this.
Beautiful trees, great lakes, and rolling hills abyss.

A simple person in this great land you see.
But as I look around, several things puzzle me.

I work hard each day trying to be free.
And not understanding why some things must be.

I labor and progress with my working desire.
Pressing hard to make things better than they really are.

My wages increase as my energy is spent.
Taxes also! And I wonder where my earnings went.

From the sweat of my brow I watch the neighbor next door.
New cars to drive, plenty to eat, and asking for more.

Tax time comes and I try for my child to deduct.
While the neighbor is having all kinds of good luck.

At the end of the year and with nothing left to give.
The neighbor and his family still have plenty to live.

The harder I work the more demands I receive.
From where I stand there appears no one to relieve.

Shall I join the ranks of those who dare?
For it appears it is those who really don't care!

How can you do this? I ask my neighbor one day!
No problem at all sir! "you see" you are paying the way!

# The Artist

From A good nights slumber I awake.
Moving about thinking of coffee to make.
To the window to see how this day will began.
I find it's quite all around, no rain, nor wind.
But there on the ground before my eyes.
Is a blanket of snow!  How beautifully it lies.
I see the clean color of white lying before me.
As if it was painted with one big brush to see.
Man paints on canvas with many strokes of the hand.
But the Master makes one stroke and paints the entire land.

# The Beauty

Picture the beauty of the morning as the day draws near.
As the light moves upon you to make the darkness disappear.
At the edge of the forest looking at the valley below.
See the beauty of the meadow with its flowering glow.
Watch as a gentle breeze moves them as the waters of the sea.
Such beauty to make the human mind wonder how it came to be.
As you sit on the green carpet made of the softest grass.
And lean against an oak tree forming questions to ask.
In the quietness of the morning, at the dawning of the day.
You will search very hard to find words to say.
To be for a whisper in time upon the gem of the universe.
To see, hear, have and to hold the beauty of God's earth.
To look into waters of its streams so crystal clear.
And walk on its hills and valleys.  Things its makers hold dear.
To look toward the eastern hills as the Sun rises above.
And see such beauty given because of love.
A gentle breeze brushes your face, as if it's trying to say.
Welcome to life my son, now relax and enjoy your stay.
What I have made I created for a reason.
Enjoy the wonders of living through your life's season.
You may not understand all you see traveling in my land.
But the pleasures will be multiplied if you hold onto my hand.
I'll be at your side as you walk, and I'll carry you if need be.
Just focus your thoughts for I am in everything you see.
All the marvels of life your eyes are allowed to behold.
Are just samples of the joys my Son has foretold.

# The Blood Shed

A thought just crossed my mind so clear and clean.
Of a man long ago that was called a Nazarene.
The story of his afflictions I am about to tell.
Mainly concerns His last hours and the blood that fell.
You see! To court they took him early one day.
A mockery they made with false words to say.
First, a scourging to his back he had to with stand.
Tearing of the flesh and his blood drips on the land.
A crown of thorns they placed on his head.
Down his face, across his cheeks, blood ran bright red.
Upon his shoulders the cross he was forced to drag.
With no one there to wipe the blood with a rag.
To the hilltop and on the cross he had to lay.
While slowly, but slowly, his blood oozed away.
Nails were driven through his hands and into his feet.
And from those wounds the blood continued to seep.
As he hung on the tree looking over everyone.
He knew the draining of his blood was almost done.
He moaned in agony while enduring such paint.
Knowing the shedding blood could be everyone's gain.
Six hours were to pass before He finished the task.
Before the flowing of his blood had run its last.
Then he gave up the spirit with a cry of agony.
For by now all his blood had drained you see.
Now some may not think very much of this story.
But if they would it could be for their own glory.
For the shedding of this man's blood, don't you see!
Allows the gift of eternal life for you and me.
Remember each time you see blood on your hand.
That Jesus the Christ was the name of this man.

# The Change

I am always amazed at the belief that the ability for
one to think and talk to themselves from the
learning's obtained throughout their lives is just
simply "talking to ones self, and yet "After" one
decides to live for the Christ and is "Baptized".
Those "Inner thoughts" that used to be "talking to
Self "now become God talking to them. No longer is it
"I thought it would be safer if I put a jack stand under the car,"
Instead it is now "God told me to put the
jack stand under the car.

# The Choice

A long time ago, when man was born.
God gave him a woman so he wouldn't be alone.
He was faced with choices that he had to take.
Some easy, some hard, but a choice he had to make.
A story of choice and the freedom of man.
As he lives his life amongst the beauty of God's land.
Not a mechanical robot that has no voice.
Just a free creation that's been given a choice.
It is really simple when it's brought to light.
His only decision is between wrong or right.
So simple it seems on what choice to make.
Just choose right or wrong and which path to take.
But he wrestles with himself, on which way to go.
He won't face the facts of what he has been told.
He is a creation of one much wiser than he.
No matter how he feels, this has to be.
A robot, he's not! To react to commands.
But free to choose, while walking this land.
A mistake he made, long, long ago.
Choosing for himself a bad way to go.
A penalty he received for the actions made.
Yet through his choice, a foundation was laid.
A test was put into motion for all mankind.
To see if he would go forward or fall behind.
The request was made and not hard to know.
Simple and fair to the one whose love he would show.
Now all the heartaches, the suffering and strife.
Are from the choices he's made throughout his life.
But from the choices he makes, I wish you to know.
They could result in great joy, if his choice is to grow.
To grow in knowledge of one greater than he.
Even to obtain life with his maker, if he chooses to be.
All joy, happiness, and life will not be lost.
If he chooses Yah, the Creator, whatever the cost.

# The City

As I sit by the river seeing the waters move swiftly by.
Watching the whirlpools form, and asking the question, why!
Why are the waters of the universe gathered in one place?
A miracle in itself to provide for the human race.
Why were the Stars made to cover the total expanse?
And the beauty of the night their lights totally enhance.
Why does the Sun sit just above the hill?
Bringing the pleasures of life in joys forever real.
Why does the trees in their luster with leaves so green.
Bring to mind a world where everything is clean?
Why is the beauty of a pasture as seen with a gentle breeze?
To picture the Lion lying with the lamb and both are at ease.
Why doesn't man believe the makers hand is in all we see?
And all things counted as bad will forever cease to be.
Why can't man in brotherly love try to do their part?
And cause the Creator to smile as joy would fill His heart.
Why can't the world be glorious and totally filled with love?
To have that loving kindness given from God above.
Why can't there be no sorrow and wars forever cease?
For the inhabitants of the earth to once more live in peace.
Why can't man believe without a shadow of doubt?
That it was because of Yah that all things came about.
Why can't we believe our king is the Son of God sent with love?
So we could live in the city that will come from the sky above.
Why can't we believe in a 1000 years of peace with the Son of man?
No want for anything for all will come from the maker's hand.

# The Cloud

As I stood and looked wishing I could fly.
I was swept away and thrown into the sky.

Having reached the end of my lofty flight.
On a fluffy white cloud I did lite.

I touched my feet on the softness of white.
With a feeling of joy and loving delight.

I reached for a rain drop from a pillar of gray.
And cast it down to go on its way.

I looked across the expanse to a cloud a far.
And wondered if that could be where the angels are.

I started to walk and jump from here to there.
Feeling the great wonders God wanted to share.

I jumped into the softness of a pillar so white.
Feeling such happiness and beautiful delight.

Looking down at the earth far, far below.
To see how the Sun made the fields glow.

How great this flight has made me feel.
To know the Creator is really real.

On the clouds of heaven I really wanted to stay.
But I knew it was a dream, so I must get under way.

But the feeling of being where God is sure to dwell.
Was enough to make me want to set sail.

To be forever with Him on the softest cloud.
Makes me be a son of whom I hope He's proud.

# The Divided Christ!

Born on the earth to give credit to the Father.
To establish a character for people to follow.
He sat an example that it could be done.
To verify the fact the Father and He were as one.
One in thought in obedience to the Fathers will.
To do so is to be found receiving the seal.
To follow the example that the Son displayed.
Is to obey the Fathers commandments without delay.
The Son did not make up his own rules for us.
He only reminded man that in the Father we can trust.
All rules from the Father were laid down.
But man has chosen not to keep them around.
To establish a route that is really not there.
Was mans way of saying that God is fair.
To worship the Father anyway is okay.
Even the move in changing the day.
To place many things before the Lord as praise.
Is changing the rules from the ancient of days.
Now the Sons teachings have been split apart.
By opinions claiming to be from the heart.
It's okay to worship as one may desire.
Raises concerns of offering a strange fire.
Now many worship in various ways.
But is it according to the ancient of days?
The world has many opinions of how it's done.
To the point they have divided the Son.
For now they state He issued new ways.
To worship him instead of the Ancient of days.
Evidence is clear and there is no doubt.
To obey the Fathers rules is what it's about.

The Son did not come to make rules of his own.
But to deliver the words from the one on the throne.
So be careful what you state in Jesus' name.]
For the Father and the Son think the same.
So to be obedient I hope you have decided.
And remember the Son is not divided.

# The Emblems

Do you have in your possession a souvenir?
Something to remind you of a thought very dear.
When you hold it in your hand from time to time.
Does it bring happy or sad thoughts to mind?
I have a few lying here and there.
That make me happy with thoughts I've shared.
There are two though! You and I can share.
Souvenirs, we call them, but emblems would be fair.
These, of course you have already guessed.
Were given to us, and are part of a test.
Once each year these emblems come in sight.
Bringing to memory and event occurring at night.
The emblems were given for us to use.
They did not give permission for us to abuse.
Given to man to share from year to year.
Given to keep in memory one very dear.
The blood and bread, is what was used.
Reminding us of life and a body abused.
Bringing to mind the one whose life was taken.
And the power of God when the earth was shaken.
This was really a true demonstration of love.
A real and sincere feeling that came from above.
A contract He (through his son) made again.
A renewed covenant, that would last to the end.
When taking of these emblems, the blood and bread.
We are reminded of the foundation formed by blood shed.
Of life-giving blood that fell on the ground.
All freely given, to bring our sins down.
Yes, as we take of these emblems, we must recall.
The events that took place that day for us all.

A reminder to us again and again.
This was freely done to relieve us from sin.
And if in seriousness of this you take.
God will grant you life and your body remake.
And as the Son said just before the end.
In our new life he will eat and drink again.
All these I am reminded from year to year.
And to sit with him at a meal is my desire to share.
To obtain the gift he has promised to give.
That is life everlasting with him to live.
So when you take of the emblems he has left to all.
Then all the events that happened you should recall.

# The Eternal Watches

The Eternal watches over the birds and provides a place for them to rest.

And He watches over those who strive to pass His test.

A test of loyalty that is offered to each under His sight.

One that provides each the chance for eternal light.

# The Fence

As the world turns daily and people play.
There is a beguilement occurring every day.
Slowly the change has been taking place.
Because sudden actions would cause an about face.
A plan the adversary long ago placed in force.
And its actions of deviation is the primary source.
Slowly but surely he is trapping his pray.
And is closing the door on many every day.
First, he places before them many actions of desire.
And as they feed on them, he sets up a fence of wire.
They express no concern and continue to eat.
While another section of fence is complete.
Thoughts of what is happening may come from time to time.
But soon the desires of the world again occupy the mind.
Warnings come from friends saying, get out without hast.
While the third section of fence around them is placed.
As they wonder from day to day with confidence they know the way.
Ignoring the evidence and what the Creator has to say.
At times the thought of being trapped may become a concern.
Yet, they ignore it because it's from man they have learned.
Before long they are again eating the desires of mans wants.
And forgetting God's word that is filled with the don'ts.
As the world turns, the fence now has become a part of life.
And the actions are accepted as part of the strife.
Soon the gate will be closed and there is no way out.
And the training is over for the adversary has removed all doubt.
Many have now become fenced and will forever remain a slave.
For the adversary has fenced them from the ancient of days.

# The Fishermen

Just as the fisherman sits in the peace
and quiet away from worries and strife.
Christ offers the opportunity for us
to escape from the sinful life.
And to a beautiful city we have the chance to go.
Where the tree of life stands
and life giving waters flow.

# The Flower

The weed grows fast and covers the ground.
The flower has hard times and usually gets beat down.
But some! Work hard and reach for the Sun.
The weed backs away so the flowers work gets done.
Its beauty is shown; the flower dies and wilts away.
It lays and waits until its resurrection day.
Then springing to life again, "Oh" it's really nice!
Especially if it is to grow forever with
Jesus Christ.

# The Hornet

The power that God gave the Hornet
to guard its home on high.
He also will give to us.
And in that, one should never deny.

To protect ourselves from the devils snare.
This He grants without a doubt.
So that when we rise from the grave
We will burst forth with the victory shout.

# The Hunter

As the hunter walks through the hills.
that are covered with a blanket of snow.
He's quickly spotted as his uniform sets the day aglow.
Just a small example of how the works of God.
Out shine everything man has made.
And tells of the Grace He had from the time
the foundation of the earth was laid.

# The Image

From deep inside come the thoughts from within.
It's our choice, whether it is real or just pretend.
In our mind we can think and feel as we desire.
They cause our actions and determine who we are.
With our mind we can be whatever we wish to be.
Even things of the future we are allowed to see.
All matter of things can be the desire of our mind.
Even the image of a friend that is loving and kind.
All types of pictures can be visible before our eyes.
Images such as the crystal streams and baby blue skies.
Yes, with our mind we can see the ones we hold dear.
We can walk and talk with anyone we wish to be near.
To place in mind the greatest friend one can ever know.
To stand beside us, and to go wherever we may go.
An image comes to mind of one we proclaim to love.
This is the Son of God who was sent by the one above.
Could we place this image always next to our side?
To go where we go or would at times He be denied?
Could He stand beside us throughout our walk in life?
To give a helping hand in our sorrows and strife.
Could we allow His image to go wherever we go?
Or would we ask Him to leave while attending a movie show?
Would we ask Him to sit beside us while talking to a friend?
Or would we refuse his company and not invite Him in?
Could we enjoy His friendship each and every day?
Or would we at times have to ask Him to go away?
This image can help us if our choice is always right.
He will be a guide while walking in the day or night.
How often to each does this image come to mind?
Is it there constantly, or just part of the time?

Does He go where we go? And stay where we stay?
Does He influence our actions each and every day?
Do we ask Him a question when we are lost in doubt?
Or just do our desire and leave Him standing about?
Each time of the day as we look for Him again.
Would we find Him with a smile or a sad grin?
Can we find Him beside us each and every time?
Or would He be in the back and walking behind?
Each day we should practice the things we proclaim.
To put in force the prayers we ask in Jesus' name.
If we can't find this image beside us the whole day through.
Then we must stop and take a good look at all the things we do.

# The Journey

The start is the first in a travel so long.
A decision that's made to choose right from wrong.
A path that is narrow and full of thorns.
That scratches and stick to the newly reborn.
Sometimes the weight of decision is a heavy load.
And one may stumble while on this road.
One may look from side to side from time to time.
And allow a shadow to cover the light that shines.
And Into a pit one can sometimes slip.
And have to look for help getting out of it.
Though that should not happen while on the way.
For the hope is to be right on judgment day.
Though shaking and anxious, one will be on this flight.
He will have to always depend on the Creators might.
With the helping hand from the one above.
One can dwell in hope based on His love.
He chose to give a chance to those who change.
And move from standard to the passing lane.
But how can one be sure they will pass?
Instead of failing and into death be cast.
In the quick sand of worldly activities one must overcome.
To do that one has to hold the hand of the begotten son.

# The Mind of Man

The mind of man has limited God all the years he has been.
And will continue, it appears, right to the very end.
When man was new, a long, long time ago.
The wisdom of God was refused in all he was told.
Man Said, "these hands God gave to help through life."
And He never intended for man to make a knife.
To cast a rock farther than an arms throw.
Is something that in this life, man will never know.
Who can invade the mind of God and think of such a thing?
Then along came a boy name David, with him came a sling.
How can it be? That from the limb of a tree.
Man can cast an arrow faster than an eye can see?
Again the thought of man started saying with a sigh.
"Man can not leave the ground" God won't let him fly!
But fly he did and with joy he would sing!
High above the clouds, riding on a steel wing.

That's it! Many said. The earth was made for man.
This is his home! No place else he will ever stand.
That is also history, for now haven't you heard,
Man stepped on the moon from out of an iron bird.
I heard yesterday, while talking to a special clan.
God will never let us make parts to replace our hand
This knowledge we have obtained even to make the human skin.
And has been to us a miracle for the benefit of men.
Steps are taken every day to move knowledge still ahead.
And they continue to say! Man will go no further" God will see him dead!
Once again we hear! To a star man will never go!
While a rocket is going to the end of our galaxy, leaving behind its glow.
The point I'm trying to make to those who hear my voice.
We can not limit God, for these things are His choice.
Man has not seen nor has he heard, all that is planed for him.
And we will continue to advance until He returns again.
If your life is long, there is no telling what you will see.
For there is no one that knows what God intends to be.
Many of us will cease to be, in the years to come.
When we do, our thoughts must be that we and Christ are one
Once again, the mind can not conceive what God has in store.
For those who have the faith and stand on the other shore.
The beauty we see while life is in our soul.
Can not compare to the beauty revealed to the ones made whole.
Our goal must be to obtain the promise Jesus Christ will give.
To see "all the things of God" is for those who forever live.

# The New Christian

I am a new Christian and I'm as happy as can be.
I've changed my life and now Christ dwells in me!
I'm new in thought and as a baby I stand.
No need to worry though, the Christians will lend a hand.
I'm glad I have Jesus! I know it's got to show.
Yet, there are many questions, the answers I've got to know!
The questions are coming quickly, trying to fill the void.
I've got to get information from the brothers about the Lord.
To one I asked a question for the answer I've got to know!
As he leaned on his rocking chair to let the story flow.
I listened intently as he made his opinions to me known.
When finished I was happy, feeling I had really grown.
To another I went, early one beautiful Sabbath day.
With joy I shared my learning, but he said it wasn't that way!
I was lost in bewilderment, as I listened to his words.
His story was much different from the other I had heard.
Opinion, it was said, is what qualifies the two.
But I was left in confusion as to which of them was true!
It doesn't make a difference, it has no bearing on eternal life.
As long as the two can share with the absence of strife.
True, I thought, as I walked toward the door.
My mind boggled down, not knowing anymore.
Lost in understanding on how each did not speak the same.
Wondering if I could continue to stay in Jesus' name.
I must listen a long time trying to understand the stories galore.
And maybe I'll understand if I reach the distant shore.
But it's going to be hard and as a newborn I must say.
I hope I don't get lost again because each story has a different way.

# The Question

Many thoughts come to mind as I behold such a wonderful sight.
My imagination runs wild, as I view the stars at night.
How can my hands move just because of a thought?
How can my legs move allowing me to walk?
What makes me awake each and every day?
What makes my mind work in its special way?
The wonders and the mysteries of how they came to be.
How is this possible? These things that surround me.
Somehow I sense a presence, and yet I cannot see!
Somehow I feel this presence is really a part of me.
Such things that happen, I can not understand.
The only answer is, these things had a helping hand.
I know that somehow, it's just got to be!
That a great designer is what has created me.
There is no other way! This I truly know.
I must believe in creation and not what I am told!

# The Reflection

Take a look at yourself in the mirror today!
Shake hands with the image being portrayed.
As you look at the reflection in the glass.
Run through your mind these questions to ask.
Is the reflection I see the reality of me?
Or does it cover the things others can't see?
Does it reflect the true feelings of "I really care?"
Or does it house evil thoughts I want to share?
Does it show an example to my neighbor friend?
Or does it allow others to know I really pretend?
Does it shine with a light as the Sun in the Sky?
Or does it show the darkness of the love I deny?
Is it a reflection that shows my belief and faith?
Or one that covers the inside of a body with hate?
Is it really a true image and likeness of Christ?
Or just a dressed up person trying to act nice.
Is it truly the likeness that it ought to be?
Or a make believe person I want others to see.
Only I can answer the question being asked!
And if I desire life I must take on this task.
In order to inherit the life the Creator has gave.
The reflection in the mirror can not have a wave.
The image I see must be a picture sin free.
Showing the Character of Christ reflected in me.
It must not show two different lives being lived!
It must show one and only one with love to give.
One should not be able to tell the two apart.
Both must show one feeling coming from the heart.
So when you look at yourself and the reflection you share.
I hope you will not see two people standing there.
For neither can inter if one is love and one strife.
Both must be the same if to obtain eternal life.
I hope what you see will all be the same.
And I hope they both will bear Jesus' name.

# The Seed

Happy, oh happy as I can be.
Two flowers my God has given to me.
From A budding seed I have watched them grow.
Now that the flowers have spread, they really glow.
Tender care must be taken daily of them.
Not to let the flowers fall from the stem.
Seeds they will spread, if it is Gods will.
And the soil of their seed they will have to till.
So I must feed them daily and water them too!
Trying to provide their needs from what is true.
For God has blessed me with these two so sweet.
A foundation I must give them made of concrete.
Teach them of the Creator God and what is true.
It is He that loaned them to me on my way through.


To Stephanie and Laura

# The Sun

The rising of the Sun with its rays so bright.

Reminds me of you as I quiver in delight.

As I look into your eyes, what do I see?

There is a sparkle I hope forever will be.

You are young now but growing very fast.

I know you can hardly wait for time to pass.

The hours, days, and years, then you will be gone.

But as long as I'm around you will never be alone.

But a man you will find and he will take my place.

And then you two will join in the worlds pace.

But remember this forever, if you need a hand.

I'll work with you and yours as best I can.

But mine, yes mine! You will always be.

As bright as the Sun and beautiful as the midday sea.

To my daughters

# The Sunset

The beauty that shows as one watches
the sun sinking in the darkness of night.

Is just a shadow of the Creators gift
through His Son that brings eternal light.

As the sun slowly sinks in the distant west.
The light is given to those who work to pass the test.

# The Third Stanza

A picture I desire to place in your mind.
Sometimes I can't because I'm left behind.

The words were placed there to convey a thought.
From time to time though, they are counted as naught.

Many times my message just can't get through.
And it's really possible; I'm trying to reach you.

All the words were recorded to tell of a way.
They are all important, with something to say.

To tell only part will only leave doubt.
It's hard to give a message when I'm left out.

Many hours in preparing the message you sing.
Why not let every one of my phrases ring.

Leaving me out does not tell the entire story.
God put me there; let me share in the glory.

Let the complete story ring out through the air.
Let me, the third stanza have a part to share.

God, I know will smile while sitting on his throne.
If we let the third stanza be a part of the song.

# The Train is Coming

There is a train coming, it's just around the bend.
It's bringing the message that time is coming to an end.
The train picks up passengers for to safely carry.
It's important enough that the people should not tarry.
The train passes through only once while on its way.
Picking up people who get on without delay.
One chance you get to make your choice.
To get on board from out of the forest.
Step on board as it's coming through.
Move quickly before it passes by you.
A ticket to travel is a must to own.
You can only obtain it from the one on the throne.
The ticket is free for the ones, who have complied.
For the price has been paid by the one that died.
So get your ticket and stand at the gate.
For the train is coming on an unknown date.

And be ready to go with your bags packed.
Filled with love for Yah, then nothing will you lack.
If the train comes and you let it go out of sight.
Rest assured you will never see the light.

# The Two hour Brother

Here I am attending church one more time.
With a smile on my face to see that brother of mine.
A pat on the back and a hand shake to show.
The kind of love all ought to know.
This smile I keep real bright and wide.
Serves a good purpose in the truth it will hide!
The fact I'm usually late I surely can't deny.
It's okay because, brotherly love is the apple of my eye.
And the pat on the back, I give to the ones I love so dear.
Is of the greatest benefit during the two hours I'm here.
Encouraging words I give to the brothers of mine.
But after parting company, I run out of time.
I feel good and leave with a wonderful attitude.
Cause I held all my anger without being rude.
And I want you to know beyond a shadow of doubt.
I can hold it in church, but soon I'm going to let it out.
It's so good to tell someone I love them!
To shake their hand, with sincerity a little slim.
Makes me feel good, doing what I'm supposed to do.
But I'm concealing anger while for two hours saying (I love you).
Yes, I tell spiritual brothers that "on me they can depend"
Then I live my life 6 days and each Sabbath make amends.
Two hours ought to be enough for one to associate.
Though that's cut short by my being late.
I do need to get a handle on this arriving on time.
For when I die I want to meet Christ, because you see!!!
I think He is a friend of mine!

# The United States Flag

*The United States Flag can serve as a reminder of Biblical Information.
The following is an example.*

It stands on a single pole and above any other flag at its side. This can remind one that there was only one God (Yah) that the forefathers gave thanks to for this country.

Its beauty of red, white, and blue colors can be compared to the Earth as seen from the moon.

**It has 13 stripes** - (6 white and 7 red) this can remind one of the 13 Apostles that Yahshua (Jesus) chose. First 12 and later Saul the 13th

**The six white stripes** - can serve as a reminder that in six days God created the heavens and the earth.

**The Seven red stripes** - can remind one that God (Yah) rested on the Seventh day and blessed it. And gave us instructions to rest every seven days.

**The color of red** - can remind one of the blood that was shed by Son of God

**The color white** - can remind one of the purity that is found in everything Yah has done. And in His Holy Spirit designed to help mankind "if allowed"

**The color Blue** - can remind one of the beauties of the heavens above.

**At this time there are 50 stars** - that can serve as a reminder that the Apostles were to wait for 50 days until the day of Penny cost. For the Holy Spirit and the ushering in of a new dispensation of promises.

**The stars are arranged in rows** — the first row has 5, the second has 4, and so it is across the banner.

**The first row of five Stars** - can remind one that Jesus fed 5 thousand from just 5 loaves of bread and two fish.

**The second row of five** - can remind one of the ten virgins - five of them were wise and five were foolish.

**The third row of five** - can remind one that Jesus gave 5 talents of money to one, two to another and one to yet another. Each according to his ability.

**The forth row of five** - can serve to remind one of the division amongst us. Five in one family divided against each other. Families divided against each other. Peace will be hard to find. And so it is with our nation.

**The fifth row of five** - can remind one of the man who made the excuse of having five yoke of oxen to care for instead of dining with Jesus. Serving as one of many excuses man will find.

**The sixth row of five** - and the end of the chain of stars can remind one of the tribulation period and how they will be tormented for having rejected God.

**The six rows of five stars total 30** - can remind one of Abraham's questioning of God to spare the cities of Sodom and Gomorrah if there were only 30 righteous people there.

**The first row of four** - can remind one that for four hundred years Israel was in bondage to Egypt.

**The second row of four** - can remind one of the second miracle of Jesus again feeding four thousand men plus women and children.

**The third row of four** - can remind us that Lazarus was dead for four days before Jesus raised him up again.

**The forth row of four** - can bring to memory the dream of clean and unclean beast that Peter had bringing an end the discrimination against each other.

**The fifth row of four** - can remind one that Jesus is coming back to gather His elect from the four corners of the earth.

**The total of the 5 rows of 4 (equal 20 stars)**- that can remind one that no one over the age of 20, (save two) were allowed to enter the promise land because of their grumbling against God after coming out of Egyptian bondage.

(Thus, serving as a reminder of the terrible fate mankind will suffer for refusing to obey God)

Compiled by **Lenvel E. Hale**

# The Volunteer Fireman

He is an every day citizen like you and me.
Not the smartest, nor best known, and may never be.
He goes about his chores as most of us do.
But ready to respond in helping me and you.
He will drop his work load at a moments end.
And come at a run with his services to lend.
In the middle of the night he will awake.
Get into his uniform and move fast for safety sake.
Floods, rains, wind, or heavy snow.
When needed, rest sure he will always show.
Why does one do this for us so freely?
Why take the gamble of hurt, to help the needy?
Is it because of publicity for himself he will ask?
"No" it's the saving of a life that he runs to the task.
It's the feeling of accomplishment he has within himself.

That he enters flaming buildings to help someone else.
It's knowing he is helping someone in deep despair.
That puts him in places others would never dare.
It's the joy of helping others that make him freely give.
And the greatest feeling is actions allowing someone to live.

# The Wind and The Spirit

The wayward wind, hear how it blows?
From where it comes no one knows.
Visions of it are hidden from the eyes.
And one will ever know where it lies.
A rush of a moment, and one feels its power.
And just as suddenly, it's gone within the hour.
Moving too and fro out of eyes sight.
Fast at times or ever so slight.
It's free indeed, as it moves around.
With a huge rumble or a whispering sound.
Freedom it's given and no boundaries lie.
To move across the surface or high in the sky.
The power it was given has a mind of its own.
Yet, directed by the Creator and Him alone.
It serves as an example of the Spirit one.
Said the Christ, when the new life has begun.
For He said we must be born again.
Born now and once more in the end.
To become invisible to the human eye.
Such is one born of the Spirit man can't deny.
And Saul said that on resurrection day.
We would be born again in a special way.
Flesh can not enter into the Spirit realm.
And we must be born of the Spirit to see Him.
A taste of the Spirit we now can receive.
But the change will come to those who believe.
When you see the evidence of the moving wind.
Remember the future holds the chance to be born again.

# The word - Love

"Oh, How I love Jesus, because he first loved me!"
Some of the best sounding words that ever came to be.
The real meaning never crossed my mind.
While I sang the song over years of time.
And today, to many such is still true.
Even when they say the words, "I love you."
"Love," "love," "love" a word only four letters long.
Yet, there is a lost meaning when it's in a song.
Nor do many transfer the feeling when sharing this word.
It's only the words "I love you," and not the feeling that are heard.
The word carries so many ways to make a person feel.
From the least of feelings to the strongest, that one can know is real.
What is this word? What makes it great?
That when applied correctly removes  the hate.
What is in it? What makes it abound?
So few letters that can make one lay their life down.
What is its meaning really to be?
Let me share these thoughts for you to see.
"L" could stand for life - the creator gave to us.
In hopes that in Him, we would put our trust.
"O" could stand for others, in whose interest we must stay.
To feel, to care, to provide a helping hand day by day.
"V" could be for victory, one shall someday feel.
If the words we say are really real.
"E" could stand for eternal. The promise granted in the end.
For the one who has the love to lay down his life for a friend.
So great this feeling, that it allows one to see.
All the good things that really ought to be.

In the love of Christ that he freely gave.
Was the feeling for another that took him to the grave.
And such today, the ultimate that one could ever feel.
If he exchanged his live for another, to receive the seal.
Love such as this is rarely shown.
For the "Ultimate" is to voluntarily trade another's life for his own.

# Thorn in the side

There are many things in life I must overcome.
If not all at once then at least one by one.

Little things were easy, they are no longer around.
Several though are still trying hard to drag me down.

Just when my mind relaxes and I feel good each day.
Along comes one of them and steps right in my way.

No matter how hard I try. This is for me a chain.
It's as a cloud over my head just to bring me pain.

I know I'm not supposed to have it. That can't be denied.
No matter how hard I try. It's surely a thorn in my side.

It effects my every action. My good deeds are wiped away.
When it comes it is so great, I sometimes forget to pray.

Everyone has a thorn, that causes struggles in life.
When it's not removed.  He is bound for a life of strife.

One thing we must know, and that beyond a doubt.
A thorn that causes sin had better be taken out.

No matter how good we are. In our daily chore.
A thorn at death, will lock us from the Saviors door.

Thorns that make us sin, are Satan's weapons of blue.
We will loose our life. And there is nothing we can do.

The essence of this story. is the question ask us all.
How important is this promise for obeying the Creator's call?

We need to think about the commandments that we are to abide.
If we value a life with Christ! Rid the thorn in the side.

The thorn in the side that causes sin is one we can control.
With it there is no eternal life. That we are told.

# Thoughts Positive

I want to enjoy myself. Just spending a day at the park!
But, I've got to leave now. It's starting to get dark.
I want to spend my time, in the light of day!
For in the darkness, I can't run and play.
But I will go home now, so I must depart!
That's if I'm lucky and my car will start.
But start it did, leaving me to wonder why.
It did not send engine parts flying in the sky!
So in this we started, to move toward home at last.
Can't go far though, without buying some high priced gas!
But have no fear, I said, "we will make it home!"
A place that cost so much, I had to take out a loan.
And so we did! As into the driveway we came.
My eyes seeing the glass from a broken window pane.
As perplexing thoughts came to me for a moment in time
"Here we go again!" got to spend more money of mine!
Into the house I was hurrying to get.
And as I sat down, the children started to fret.
Oh! For relaxing moments, why can't they belong to me?
Why is it that all bad things, seem always mine to be?
Surely in the toils of life, there is something good to share.
My eyes see the worst and it's sometimes hard to bear.
God let my mind see the goodness in your way.
As the thoughts came to me on the events of the day.
A smoothing comfort came over me, as I felt Him say.
Don't worry about it getting dark, be happy you can play!
Rather than concern about a car that may not run!
Be happy, for some people do not have even one.
Instead of being amazed, the engine didn't come apart!
Be happy to have one that will drive you to a park.

And instead of the cost of fuel invading your thoughts!
Why not be thankful for the last fuel that you bought?
Instead of resentment for having a loan to repay!
Be thankful to God that your family has a place to stay.
Instead of allowing thoughts of madness to come over you!
Remember, during ones life, some things will make one blue.
And finding faults in the children over small arguments!
Be thankful, for to some these little ones are never sent.
Instead of looking for the negative in things you do and say!
Reach for the positive in every event of the day.
Be glad in what God allows, these things can make us strong!
Giving us strength to someday, with Christ sing a new song.
All things happen for a cause, either pro or con.
To understand why, requires between God and man a bond.
So when you start to find fault and your smile goes away.
Think on Christ and the positive, for it will make your day.

# """"Tick Tock"""""

I will say! Except Christ today!
You will wait, doing your way.
Don't you know the call is nearing?
We must labor hard, and must help the erring!
Time is running out! We must work without delay!
Because many souls will be lost on that day!
I will move now! For I've got to do my part.
Hope you will too! Only you know your heart!
Tick Tock, goes the clock, moving the hands of time.
Each breath we take! each beat of the heart!
Is measuring yours and mine.
Let's work hard for Christ before we rest.
Then we can say on that day.
I know I have passed the test!

# Tis a sad but true story

Tis a sad but true story and from the world it came.
How Jesus is dead and everything's the same.
Together in this world, it's up to each to take or give.
Each is to determine their life, and the way they live.
To rule is for man to have total control.
It's not relinquished to anyone! This we are told.
Living in a world today, that requires many choices.
Those who speak the loudest seem to have the voices.
Yield to the screams that demand changes for today.
The question of right or wrong, are not to get in the way.
The standard that once guided everyone to the light.
Has slowly been pushed aside, and replaced with the night.
No power is needed, but the one that we call ours.
And we choose the destiny that meets our own desires.
It's a sad but a true story, and from the world it came.
It has brought man to the point of global shame.
He murders, rapes, and steals from everyone.
His conscience has been seared to the point he has none.
Some still claim to hold the values that came from the old.
But the world sees no difference except what they are told.
For most who claim to live their lives in the light.
Are really casting shadows that belong in the night.
It's a sad but true story and from the Bible it came.
That after a period of time, all would be the same.
Man would forget the past that told the story of love.
Changing the relationship with a Creator until it's push and shove.
But the story is not erased, no matter how hard it's tried.
We still have the words of one who can't be denied.
There is still a foundation as solid as a rock.
And it can't be changed for it doesn't contain a clock.
It gives one peace of mind in knowing this world is only the start.
Of a vision of another life, in which a few will have a part.
It's a glad and true story - and from the Bible it came.
Eternal life is promised to those obedient to the Fathers  name.

# Tis the time of the year

Tis the time of the year when leaves start to fall.
Lying on the ground waiting for the tree to recall.

Tis the time of the year for the cold to come.
Taking away the warmth bringing chills to everyone.

Tis the time of the year for the snow to fall.
Bringing the minerals to the soil to benefit us all.

Tis the time of the year when Pagan rule will rein.
In sheep's clothing to bring sorrow and pain.

Tis the time of the year many untruths shall unfold.
During the season when Christ birth is being told.

Tis the time of the year of worshipping the birth of the seed.
And commands shall be forgotten because of this deed.

Tis the time of the year when Satan shall strut down the aisle.
Because of lives being lost to traditions that beguile.

# To Late

He hears the call of "to dinner come"
There's no need to hurry, no need to run.
His time he took, he knew they will wait!
As he came through the door, he was late.

To the store He is to go to obtain a few.
He will take his time, just a couple things to do.
Then to the store for the things he had to get.
To his surprise, he found there was no bread to let.
The excess time that he did take.
Had caused him to arrive just a little too late.

He heard about a person that was in great need.
This was his chance to do for someone a good deed
What was needed in this cause, he was not sure.
But for the time he took. The person will have to endure.
He'll not be in a hurry, He knows the help can wait.
But when he arrived. He was a little too late!

To Church he goes, each Sabbath day.
He doesn't get there on time cause things get in the way.
He is always forgetting, either the time or the date.
And because of this, he is always a little late.

Living his life to perfection he feels can't be done.
For when looking for sin. He always finds one.
He will get it removed, but for now it will have to wait.
He will be careful and make his mends just a little before it's too late.
Last night he died and today he stands before the throne.
Finding himself with sin and standing all alone.
Of all the times he should have hurried, he put it off for a later date.
Now he finds that for eternal life, he is also just a little too late!
Let this story be a lesson for your future slate.
Don't put obedience off or you could find it will be a little too late!

# Traditions of old

The traditions of old and how they sway.
Causing the false belief we face today.

An example I'll share as you read these lines.
For contained within them the truth you'll find.

As the story goes that caused the Ark to float.
Saying Noah spent 120 years to build the boat.

Working hard through the agony and pain.
Even though it's said he had never seen a rain.

It was faith in God that made him work.
Spending all those years on dry dirt.

The story that's heard is really not true.
That until the flood God only watered with the dew.

It's true that the dew was used to water the land.
But, that was before the making of man!

They say that the rain came and the boat did float.
Causing the world to take note.

It came to rest on a mountain they now say.
All in an attempt for the truth to sway.

For the Bible is true with its information fountains.
That tell us it came to rest in a group of mountains.

This is just one story that we have been told.
That comes to us from the traditions of old.

A story that's changed from the recorded word.
To form a story where the truth is not heard.

As you listen to the stories you are being told.
Make sure they are not a tradition of old.

# We need a Volunteer

We need a volunteer! The question is posed.
And from the crowd the rich man rose.

I'll give of my means was his quick reply.
For on what I have left I can rely.

If I give to help I will still have much left.
I won't have to worry about supporting myself.

This is the cheerful giver we usually find today.
For it's easy to give when it doesn't get in our way.

We need a volunteer! The question is posed.
This time all was quite because no one rose.

Who will give to help a loved one on this lovely day?
The crowd was silent, No one would say.

Why not give to help the needy get along?
Again was the question stated.
All was still while everyone waited.

Surely there is one who has something to give!
But this crowd needed all they had in order to live.

While plenty abounds and one feels safe for sure.
It is then they will give a little to help others endure.

But when threatened of losing that which is near.
Thoughts of preservation will start to appear.

The Scriptures tell of a woman that gave two pennies.
And she had nothing left while others would not give any.

To give what you have and have nothing to remain.
Is like the love of Christ when he allowed his blood to drain.

When one has plenty it is easy to share with another. The thought of being without doesn't come to mind. The average income person has a different outlook on the situation. Sharing is something they have to work at because it means one must plan ahead to be sure they have enough to provide the things needed. The poor person is placed in a different category. This one has no means of real support. Giving to another means they must do without. It means watching another go away with the necessities of life while placing oneself in the position of non existence. Christ said that "greater love has no man than to lay down his life for another" This is the ultimate giving. A poor person that will have nothing left once it is given away. Compared to other parts of the world is still rich. We live in an abundance of food, clothing, campers, homes, land, you name it we have it It is easy to say we will do something when in the back of our minds we really do not believe we will have to do it. It's easy to say we would die rather than deny Christ when we really feel that in this country that will not come about. The Military makes the soldier practice ramming another with a bayonet over and over again and again. This is to condition them to do it naturally without thinking if the real situation should occur. We must practice over and over again in our minds that we will not deny Christ should it become a reality. And I must add! That denying Christ does not only come in the phrase from someone "deny Christ" It comes in our actions and deeds also.

# We Say!

He can form the mountains or a thousand hills.
Or make the stars of the Universe and anchor them still.

We say! He can raise us from the dead long after we are gone.
And grant us eternal life and make the earth our home.

We say! He can heal our bodies from sickness and death.
Or grant us favors that bring us wealth.

Then we say! One will sin from day to day.
For he can't make a set of laws man can obey.

# What God are you talking about?

Because of our countries continued violation of the commandments of our Creator in which He said "You shall have no other gods but me!" I am compelled to ask a question! The continued emphasis on our asking <u>God</u> for help. Or making statements such as, we are sowing a seed to <u>God,</u> or stating we are sending a seed for <u>God!</u> Makes it necessary for me to ask.

### <u>What God are you talking about?</u>

I am aware one can quickly state "there is only one God" and they would be right in the sense there is only one true God. But the Scriptures state there are gods many. And in the mind of the people of the world that is true for they call upon the names of many gods. It is sad that most of the Christian world does not personally know our Creator. And it is also sad they continue to place him in the same ranking with other gods by refusing to address Him personally. This is done my many as a result of not having heard or choosing not to hear that He has an identity. It appears to be very clear that in His recorded word He intended to be known by a name for He left it over 6025 times. Satan, has attempted to take away the personality of our Creator, to bring Him down to the level of the unknown god. For His name has been brought to nothing. And that in itself is a violation of His third commandment. Many fall into the trap of arguing that the way to pronounce His name is not known and therefore shy away from it. However, I would like to share that man calls His name today without even knowing it. In that they say "Hallelujah" which actually means "Phrase ye Yah" Even in the Greek language in which the New "renewed" Testament was written one finds the word Alleluia and it has the very same meaning of "Phrase ye Yah". One can also find the name "Yah" throughout the Psalms. Therefore I submit that we can have a better relation with Him by calling upon Him personally. If one thinks they are being blessed by addressing him as God then try addressing him personally. And as the old saying goes,

### "You ain't seen nothing yet!"

# What kind of a life do we live?

What kind of a life do we live?
In this world of sorrow, what kind of love do we give?

Heartaches abound amongst the people we know.
What kind of friendship do we show?

We are in the world, and of the world we should never he.
What kind of an example do we set for another to see?

Life is short- it's a whisper that will come to pass.
What kind of foundation have we laid? How long will it last?

From the valleys low to the mountains high.
On what kind of friend do we rely?

These words are written to bring to mind.
What kind of memories will we leave behind?

After our life here is through.
What kind of future will come into view?

# What would we do if Jesus was among men?

What would we do if Jesus was here again?
If He did the same as when He first began?

How would we act hearing our faults told?
Would we listen with love or would we scold?

If He were to tell us we were wrong with a thought.
Who would be the first to bring His words to a halt?

If He appeared on television speaking to a crowd.
Would our disagreeing change to a voice ranging loud?

If He were to say, the Sabbath is not to bind.
Who would be the first to speak their mind?

Who would invite this one for dinner to stay?
In hopes their belief could his mind sway.

With all the "right" points we have heard.
Do you think anyone would take his word?

Would you know it was Christ speaking to you?
If you felt what He said was untrue.

Yes, today like yesterday, all have their belief.
Today like yesterday, would we place on him grief?

Would He have to say for us as He did them?
Forgive them father! I will be their friend!

# What's going to happen when I die?

As I stand in the middle of the night, looking at the Stars in the sky.
I'm filled with the powerful thoughts.

"What's going to happen when we die?"

As I stand in a field and look at the mountains that surround.
The demonstration of power so great I can only hang my head down.
As I look at the wonders of the clouds that form in a clear sky.
I'm lost in the beauty of white, and again the question.

"What's going to happen when we die"?

As I stand in the forest and watch the waters of a crystal stream go by.
The reflection I see, the image so real brings again the question,

"What's going to happen when we die"?

Yes, what's going to happen when we die? A question always raised.
Where do we go? What is it like? Comes this question from ancient days.

A lost feeling comes over me. It's the darkness of the grave we fear.
Just to lay there, and to be alone, to not have anyone be near
Is there any comfort for us? That we may loose this fear and dread?
Then I remember! There are words recorded saying one can be raised from
the dead!

Who can give this inner feeling of security for life again for one to see?
Who has the power to turn my dust into a form and give this life to me?

There must be someone who can save us so we may lay in peace
Jesus Christ! I've read has this power to grant to us this release,

What must we do to obtain that which can be granted to us?
The words say, have faith, obey God, and put Christ as our trust.

It's the actions toward faith in Christ on which we can rely.
That will remove the agonizing question of old.

"What's going to happen when we die"?

# Where are you Lord, where have you gone?

Where are you Lord?  Where have you gone?
I've looked everywhere and you aren't shown.

I've looked through the forest to find you there.
I walked the mountains and though the valleys fair.

I flown over the clouds and all it seems in vain.
I've hidden in the closets and called your name.

I roamed in the darkness and hoped to find you there.
To the watery depths as far as I would dare.

I've run to and fro searching desperately.
And all I see in my efforts is a lonely me.

I know I've been told you were everywhere.
And if I really looked I could find you there.

Where are you Lord?  Why do you hide yourself?
Please help me for thoughts are all I have left.

Are you in the trees that are ever so green?
Or in the clear waters of a crystal stream?

Are you in the clouds that move across the land?
Or in the breeze as it sifts the sand?

Are you in the heavens that are far above?
Or in the depths of the word love?

Where are you Lord?   Please make me see.
That you are in everything including me.

# Where did I come from?

Was I born out of the miry clay?
Or was I an accident that occurred one day?
Were my arms formed and placed on me?
Or did I grow them as a product from the sea?
Are my legs a design of a plan complete?
Or were they formed from a creature from the deep?
Did my heart begin to beat because of a plan?
Or did it accidentally form from a creature on land?
Can I walk because someone designed it so?
Or did they accidentally form so I could go?
And my mind - Where did it come from?
Was it something that happened like my finger and thumb?
But most of all, there is something I don't understand.
How can an accident occur to form the mind of man?
Accidents happen in this world from time to time.
But to give us a spirit of thought coming from the mind.
Is like throwing the Alphabet up in the air.
To form the Dictionary for us to share.
Can the 26 letters falling to the ground.
Form the thousands of words that we have around?
I am a product of design from a master's hand.
And not from Evolution as some understand.
When we look at ourselves with our hands and feet.
There should be no doubt we are a plan complete.

# Where did the years go?

As a child with no cares nor need to be concerned.
It's easy to forget time required for lessons learned.
And as the days go by with an easy flow.
*Never the question, where did the years go?*
As a young adult under the guidance of home.
With constant yearning and desires to roam.
To church each week one may always go.
To change actions that may never show.
Responsibilities to belong one will continued to shun.
Paying no attention as a new year has begun.
From school to college for the diploma to show.
*Yet, never the question, where did the years go?*
A mate one can have and children for a treat.
Young at heart with responsibilities to meet.
Looking at signs of creation on display.
Yet avoiding Yah to choose their own way.
Busy working to accumulate material wealth.
Neglecting to put first their eternal health.
Absent are the thoughts of reward or woe.
*And never the question - where did the years go?*
Then comes the time of old and getting gray.
Looking at the future and the years on the way.
The actions of their past and the choices took.
The dust on the bible of which they never look.
Remembering the times that the Creator reached down.
Yet instead of following, they had turned around.
Now seeing the way He wanted them to know.
*Suddenly, the question - where did the years go?*
Waiting until one is old, feeble and weak.
And there is no energy for which to seek.

That which was wasted in the youthful years.
Has now been replaced with wishful tears.
Though it's not too late to make the new start.
Remember along with age comes the hardness of heart.
Please let these words sink deep within your ear.
Don't take the chance of wasting a year.
For life will pass by with you wanting to know.
***And always the question! Where did all the years go?***

# Which Way Will He Point?

I 'm awake and yet! Darkness surrounds me.
I 'm lying in a box! But how can this be?
"I remember!" the brake squeal, with all the frightening sound.
The sudden force. The breaking glass, my landing on the ground.
The lights dimmed, people gathered around, as my thoughts begin to fade.
Now I know! I have died! And in this coffin I was laid.
But how is this? That I'm awake with sounds all around.
Wait a minute! Something's happening! I'm moving through the ground!
Now I am standing on top, and I see people everywhere.
They are acting very strange, I speak, but they don't seem to hear.
In the distance I see a crowd and there is a light over head.
I'm uncertain, but compelled to see where they are being lead.
As I approach, I see a man and there is a glow all around.
Then I know! It's Jesus Christ! As my knees touch the ground.
He is moving his hand left and right, causing people to separate.
Then I realized, one side was love, and the other side was hate.
Now I know why I'm alive, for this is the judgment day.
This is the day I was told my past would be measured every way.
A frightening comes over me as I move closer to his throne,
As I tremble from my past, I ask myself, who's side was I really on?
I've known Christ, and went to church through out all my years.
Shaking now, I know I'm dead, so how can my eyes be full of tears?
What is He going to say when I stand and look straight at Him?
Will He say welcome Brother! To my right, or "you go with them!"
In times past I've left Him out and tried to handle things alone.
He wanted help, but it's too late for now I'm approaching His throne.
He's right there! So close to me! Dressed in a remnant of pure white.
Fear has a grip on me; will He point to the dark or to the light?
I see my life pass before me, and all my past is made known.
If I could do it over again, more love I would have shown.

Of the many times, and the many deeds that I could have done.
Was it enough? Did I have Christ? Eternal life have I won?
I used to say. Come on back Lord! I'm ready for you!
But now I'm here, with fear and trembling. Was I really true?
It's my turn now, as He turns and looks, pointing at me!
I almost faint with the Question, which way will His pointing be?
Then, with a sudden jump I sat up in bed, alone and so afraid.
A pounding heart and shaking hands, happy I'm not in the grave.
I must make sure that when I die and again I see the light.
What I will see, is a smile on Christ, with his finger pointing to the right!

# Whisper the Truth to Me

Hear this! Hear this! Hear what I have to say!
The Churches this fits will fall on judgment day!
Mans thoughts and mans deeds you have put first!
Changing Gods commands until now it has gotten worse.
You claim to be right in all you say and do.
While constantly you are breaking His golden rule!
Don't worry about tomorrow, only today!
Yet continue to put worldly things in the way.
But worldly things you say you do not need,
While buying land, an only for greed.
Come worship with us and become a part!
Profit you are after, it is not from your heart!
If God's interest were your desire!
You would change the way you really are!
Stop running around and make some corrections!
Get together and issue the same directions.
Get with each other and find the true way,
Give people the true story of eternal life today!
Then maybe, yes maybe, God will show,
All the churches the correct way to go.
I am here in agony looking to and fro.
Everyone says (here is truth) but I don't know.
A bible scholar I know I shouldn't have to be!
But you have twisted the word and I must be to see.
God, I hope will have mercy on you.
For not telling the people what is really true.
For eternal life from many you have stole,
Because all the time your interest was in gold.
It is the innocent and uneducated I am sorry for on that day.
They depended on you and you lead them astray!

There is a place reserved for the ones like you!
That lives a lie and yet proclaim it to be true.
Wake up! wake up! And get your story straight.
Start leading the people toward the narrow gate.
If not then mercy, mercy, you will cry.
While in your ears the words, Thou shall surly die!

# Who am I?

I watched a little boy today.
Having a real hard time trying to play.
Jolly was he. With a smile on his face.
Pushing a toy and trying to race.
He jumped and shouted from shear joy.
Laughing and giggling as his mom handed the toy.
As I watched him try again and again.
Just stopping to look now and then.
My eyes filled with tears and I even lost my speech.
For the little guy had no arms in which to reach.
Even move he made was as though to say.
"I can get along each and every day."
As 1 reached to pick up a toy and give to him.
He looked up at me with this huge grin.
And though he had no arms in which to rely.
Thank you sir! Was this little guys reply.
As he turned and tried to lift the toy with his feet.
I felt warmth as my heart skipped a beat.
Happiness seemed to abound because his smile had a shine.
And 1 couldn't help feeling pain in my mind.
When I look at my hands that move to and fro.
And my feet that take me where I desire to go.
<u>Who am I.</u> to find fault with my little aches and pains?
or to be angry because of no earthly gains.
Who am I to question when I feel blue?
For when I need my arms. 1 have two.
They obey my command whenever I wish.
For the hard to get or just a simple dish.
Who am I to feel sorry for my small areas of defeat?
For without his arms he chooses not to be beat.

Who am I to get angry within my living years?
When I can watch him play without shedding a tear.
As the little boy turned to move the toy with his feet.
My heart became so heavy I started to weep.
Weeping with feelings of sadness for the little guy.
I have to ask and wonder. Who am I?
He acts and plays as though there was nothing wrong.
Who am I. to question how he sings his song?
God allows things to occur even though we wonder why.
But to question His reasons.
Who am I?

# Why can't we?

As I sit by the river watching the waters move swiftly by.
Seeing the whirlpools form and asking the question. Why?

Why are the waters of the universe gathered in one place?
A miracle in itself to provide for the human race.

Why were the Stars made to cover the total expanse?
And the beauty of the night their lights totally enhance.

Why does the Sun sit just above the hill?
Bringing the pleasures of life in joys forever real.

Why does the trees in their luster with leaves so green?
Bring to mind a world where everything is clean.

Why does the beauty in a pasture seen with a gentle breeze?
Picture the Lion laying with the Lamb and both being at ease.

Why doesn't man believe the makers hand is in all we see?
And all things counted as bad will forever cease to be.

Why can't man in brotherly love try to do their part?
And cause the Creator to smile as joy would fill his heart.

Why can't the world be glorious and totally filled with love?
To have that loving kindness given from Yah above.

Why can't there be no sorrow and wars forever cease?
For the inhabitants of the earth to once more live in peace.

Why can't man believe without a shadow of doubt?
That it was because of Yahweh that all things came about.

Why can't we believe our king is the Son of God sent with love?
So we could live in the city that will come from the sky above.

Why can't we believe in the desire of peace from the Son of man?
That man was placed on earth to love and enjoy the land.

Why can't we love our brother by obeying our makers command?
Then the want for nothing, for all would come from the maker's hand.

# Why?

An amazing and wonderful thing happened last night:
I dreamed of the Creator and His awesome might.
Of standing and looking into the darkness of the sky.
To gaze at the beauty, and to wonder "Why!"
Lost in thought, I felt sudden chills travel over me.
To stand on this earth, to walk through the trees, or wade at the edge of a sea.
Questions come to mind, "What if I could move from here to there?"
Plant my feet on a star, to see all the Creator is willing to share.
To walk on the surface of the moon and leave my foot-prints in the soil.
To stand on its mountain tops to view another part of God's labor and toil.
To travel from there to the closest planet, anchored in space for all to see.
And visualize having a part that God would give to me.
I imagined walking on an asteroid as it circled around a star.
Sitting and watching as the earth went by, to be where the angels are.
Taking one giant leap to the stars of the Milky Way.
To see another part of creation promised to man someday.
Jump after jump, place after place, to the edge of the universe I came.
Looking across the great expanse, to another solar system called by name.
On and on, from one galaxy to another, I continued to fly.
Passing such wonders of creation, causing the never ending question of,
"Why?"
I stood in the middle of it all, and no end could I see.
The greatness of the universe, the mystery of how it came to be.
My mind could not conceive all that He had made.
As no man can know why the foundation was laid.
I only know I was there and it was a part of God's plan.
I only know He has offered for me to hold His hand.
The joy in my dream I can not explain to you.
Nor can I give you the feelings, only to say they were true.
How it is possible, a Creator could do for us what He has done?

To show the love for man by the actions of His only Son.
All for a chance to move throughout the empty space.
Makes me still wonder, why did He choose the human race?
Maybe someday you too can dream the dream that came to me.
And then you can see the awesome beauty, I was allowed to see.
Yet, now that I am awake -1 stand and gaze into the sky.
And the continued question races through my mind, and I still wonder

**"Why?"**

# Words of wisdom

I remember the Family Bible that used to sit on the shelf.
It's the only original book that I kept for myself.
I remember the times my mom and dad would read from its pages.
And tell me the stories that happened throughout the ages.
Those times have fond memories as I recall how dad used to say.
Son, there is wisdom in these pages to guide you along the way.
And as I grew older, a teenager I came to be.
Not as often did I sit for dad to read to me.
And now dad and mom are gone and I seldom read the book.
Because amongst its pages I really don't want to look.
Instead, the family Bible sits waiting to be heard.
Standing as a monument of Gods recorded word.
Handed down through generations until it came to me.
Its pages only wrinkled by those interested enough to see.
Though I often desire to seek from the information contained within.
I continue to pass it by and listen to others tell about my sin.
Why the need to open the book when from others I hear the way.
Instead I will pass a prized possession down the family chain someday.
Now time has come and gone and I have let it go slipping by.
Absent from my mind are God's words I can't deny.
Yes, the time is almost gone and I wonder if I understand.
Have I truly been living right from the instructions given by man?
The answer I need to know before my life comes to a close.
Will I obtain life eternal or another path have I chose?
As my trembling hands reach for the book still placed within the case.
I suddenly realize that in obeying, my life has been a waste.
For contained within the pages are the instructions to take a stand.
But they have all been traded by hearing the words spoken by man.
I passed up opportunities after the Bible was given to me.
Now the light grows dimmer as my eyes have failed to see.
If I had a word of wisdom for all to hold near.
Never let another tell what they want you to hear.
For life could pass you by until you're old and gray.
Leaving you standing alone not knowing what God had to say.

# Young Ones

Oh youthful ones of today! Such running about you try to do.
While the works of the Lord you're turning away.
Why not learn the Lords way? For it is true.
Thousands of years of knowledge wait to unfold.
All the ways of happiness waiting to be told.
Such thrills you believe you get from drugs at times.
But with things like that there is no way to become kind.
Learning from others experience has always been told.
Is a sign of maturity and wisdom one can behold.
Love is the key to a great world for us.
Not moving back and forth, wanting for lust!
Love for you and love for me wouldn't that be nice?
And you know! The only way to achieve it,
is through Jesus Christ

# You're the one

You're the one that spoke and formed the clear blue sky.
And you're the one who made the birds in the heavens fly.

You're the one who made the grass grow on a given day.
And you're the one that caused changes just from what you say.
You're the one that formed man from the dust of the ground.
And you're the one that made the woman for him to be around.

You're the one that loved so much to cause your son to meet his fate.
And come into a world that was filled with jealous and hate.
You're the one who formed everything man has seen or heard.
You're the one who made all things by your spoken word.

You're the one who gave me hope from a life of despair.
You're the one who processed a son that you desired to share.
And you're the one who has provided a means for another life.
One that will be absent of all sorrow and strife.

You're the one who gave all you had for me.
You're the one that directed him to be nailed to a tree.
Yes you're the one that had your word buried to come alive again.
And you're the one that had him pay for all the human sins.
Yes you're the one! You're the one! You're the one!

# Dee

As the blue of the water is meant to be.
My love for you is for all to see.

As solid as the rock we are sitting on.
My desire is for us to always be one.

Side by side as I sit always next to you.
Joys to share while on our way through.

As the waters are deep and crystal clear.
The sparkle never fades holding you near.

Love of life is the greatest joy one may find.
The pleasures are magnified because you are mine.

May the joys of togetherness never be swayed.
And the beauty always seen in what God has made.

May you always be mine.

To my wife Dee.

Lenvel E.  Hale

# Table of Contents